The "Fuero Militar" in New Spain

1764 - 1800

The "Fuero Militar" in New Spain

1764 - 1800

by

LYLE N. McALISTER

UNIVERSITY OF FLORIDA PRESS

Gainesville

1 9 5 7

A University of Florida Press Book

Library of Congress Catalogue Card No. 57–10614

PRINTED BY THE H. & W. B. DREW COMPANY
JACKSONVILLE
FLORIDA

Preface

S OME YEARS AGO, I undertook a study of the organization and expansion of the Army of New Spain in the last decades of the eighteenth century. As research progressed, it became more and more obvious that the real importance of the army lay not in its role as an instrument of national defense but in its impact on existing civil institutions. The present volume is a study of one aspect of this problem, the disruptive effects of the legal privileges and immunities enjoyed—and abused—by the colonial army. In a broader sense it is a study in the origins of civil-military relations in independent Mexico, for military privilege outlived the viceroyalty. It was part of the colonial heritage that survived in a virulent form to plague the republic.

The publication of this work would not have been possible without generous assistance from many sources. I deeply appreciate grants from the Henry L. and Grace Doherty Charitable Foundation and from the Penrose Fund of the American Philosophical Society, which enabled me to use the resources of Mexican archives. I will always remember the courtesy and cooperation of the staff of the Archivo General de la Nación. I am indebted to Professor Lawrence Kinnaird of the University of California at Berkeley who first suggested the possibilities of a study of the military reorganization of the Spanish colonies. Professors Lesley Byrd Simpson and Woodrow Borah, also of the University of California at Berkeley, submitted the manuscript to relentless criticism. Finally, I wish to thank Professor Donald Worcester who, as head of the History Department at the University of Florida, encouraged my work in ways too numerous to mention.

L. N. McA.

Contents

ONE

Introduction

T HE RESULTS of the Seven Years' War brought to a climax the efforts of the Spanish Bourbons to reform the administration of their empire. During that struggle Spain and France suffered humiliating reverses in colonial theaters of operation, and both powers nursed a desire for revenge and the recovery of territorial losses. Both, moreover, feared that England would not be satisfied with her gains and soon would attempt to expand her possessions at their expense. Consequently, the partners in the Family Compact exerted every effort to prepare themselves for the next phase of the struggle which they regarded as inevitable.[1]*

An integral part of their plans was the strengthening of the Spanish overseas possessions so that they could not only defend themselves but could also make substantial financial contributions to imperial defense. The Spanish crown and its French advisers agreed that this could be accomplished only by a thorough overhaul of the old colonial system. From this conclusion grew the series of administrative and fiscal reforms associated with the reign of Charles III (1759–1788).[2] These included the preliminary visitations of José de Gálvez and José Antonio de Areche to New Spain and Peru, respectively, the expulsion of the Company of Jesus from the Americas, the introduction of the intendant system into the colonies, and the establishment of "free trade" within the empire. In addition, strenuous efforts were made to stimulate important colonial industries. In New Spain, for example, the tobacco industry was reorganized as a royal monopoly and a mining guild was created with extensive control over mining operations and litigation.[3]

A more direct approach to the problem of imperial defense lay in the strengthening of the overseas military establishments. Before the Seven Years' War these were hardly more than token. In 1758 there were in New Spain only some 3,000 regulars who were employed almost exclusively in garrison duty on the northern frontier and

*Chapter notes begin on page 16.

1

in the principal ports (see Table 1, Appendix I). This force was supplemented by a colonial militia. In the Spanish military organization two important classes of militia existed, the provincial and the urban. The prototype of the provincials was thirty-three regiments of infantry formed in thirty-three provinces of Castile. This class was also known as "disciplined" militia because the regiments had a standard organization, received systematic training, and were provided with a cadre of regular officers and enlisted men.[4] In New Spain, however, disciplined provincial units had never been formed. Instead, there existed throughout the viceroyalty a number of separate companies of infantry and cavalry (see Table 1, Appendix I). These had no uniform organization and for the most part were understrength, untrained, and lacked arms, uniforms, and equipment.[5]

Urban units were formed in the larger cities and in strategically located coastal and frontier towns. As a rule they were sponsored by the municipal corporations or by the guilds of the communities. Only in times of the greatest emergency were they summoned into active service, and then only for the defense of the immediate locality.[6] In New Spain, urban militia existed in Puebla and Mexico. In the latter city the consulado manned and supported the Regiment of Commerce; two companies of cavalry were sponsored by the guilds of pork-butchers, bakers, and tanners; the silversmiths' guild supported a company of infantry; and a regiment of infantry was maintained by the *cabildo*. In Puebla the merchants supported a regiment of infantry, and the guilds of pork-butchers, bakers, and tanners sponsored a company of cavalry (see Table 1, Appendix I). The function of these troops was to guard and police their respective cities in cases of emergency.[7]

The militia of New Spain was drawn from all classes of population except Indians. Units composed of personnel of pure Spanish blood were classified as *blanco* or *español*, and those made up of persons of mixed Spanish and Indian descent as mestizo or *castizo*. There were also companies of mulattoes, *morenos* (pure Negroes), and *pardos* (literally speaking, the offspring of free Negro parents).[8] The term *pardo*, however, was commonly employed in a broader sense to include all persons of Negro or part-Negro blood. In the interest of simplicity this usage will be employed throughout this study.[9] It should be added that the classification of militia by caste or color cannot be taken too literally. By the middle of the eighteenth century miscegenation had proceeded so far that distinctions based entirely on purity of blood or on kind and degree of blood mixture were impossible to maintain. Instead, an individual's caste or status tended to depend on his social or economic position, and many persons with Indian or Negro blood passed as *blancos* or *españoles*. Indeed, most of those who were not of "color achocolatado" regarded themselves, and in practice were regarded, as *españoles*.[10] It is probable, therefore, that many units designated as *blanco* contained a high proportion of mixed bloods.

The reverses suffered by Spain during the Seven Years' War highlighted the inadequacy of overseas military establishments. To meet the problem a secret committee for imperial defense was organized in Madrid, and early in 1764 this body presented the outlines of a comprehensive plan. One of the most important of the committee's recommendations provided for the creation of colonial armies. The nuclei of these forces were to be regular troops of two classes; first, *fijo* units—that is, regiments and battalions raised and stationed permanently in the colonies—and second, Spanish units which were to rotate in overseas service. Considerations of economy, however, made it impracticable to maintain enough regulars in America to bear the burden of defense alone. The mass of the armies was to consist of colonial militia, greatly augmented in strength and organized on a disciplined footing like the provincials of Castile.[11]

The implementation of the program in New Spain was entrusted to Lieutenant General Juan de Villalba y Angulo, then captain general of Andalusia. Villalba arrived in Veracruz in November, 1764, accompanied by the Regiment of Infantry of America, newly recruited in Spain, as well as by cadres of officers and men for the formation of new regular and provincial units.[12] During the first months of his mission, the general completely reorganized the regular troops of the viceroyalty. The existing infantry and mounted units of Veracruz and Mexico were deactivated and their personnel either discharged or incorporated into the Regiment of America and two new mounted regiments of the *fijo* class, named the Regiment of Dragoons of Spain and the Regiment of Dragoons of Mexico. Thus the regular component of the Army of New Spain was initially established at one regiment of infantry, two of dragoons, and miscellaneous service and presidial troops (see Table 2, Appendix I). Villalba next turned his attention to the militia, and by August, 1766, he and his assistants had raised six regiments and three separate battalions of provincial infantry and two mounted regiments of the same class. In addition, the Lancers of Veracruz and the companies of *pardos* and *morenos* of that city were incorporated into the new provincial establishment, and the urban units of Mexico and Puebla were reorganized but retained their urban status (see Table 2, Appendix I).[13]

During the next fifteen years the Army of New Spain underwent further growth. In 1767 Viceroy the Marqués de Croix increased the strength of the regular dragoon regiments and raised an infantry regiment of the *fijo* class, christened the Regiment of the Crown of New Spain.[14] The Regiment of America returned to Europe in 1769, but was replaced, in accordance with the Spanish policy of rotation, by the second battalions of the regiments of Saboya, Ultonia, and Flandes.[15] Spanish regiments continued to serve in the viceroyalty until they were finally replaced in 1787 by newly formed *fijo* troops.[16]

In regard to the provincial militia, the initial formation was somewhat less than successful. When Croix assumed office in 1766 he found that the units raised by Villalba were understrength; many of the enlisted personnel lacked the physical qualifications for military service or were burdened with large families; some units had no officers; no training program was established; troops were without arms, uniforms, or equipment; and no adequate provisions existed for financing the militia program.[17] Croix tried to remedy these deficiencies by reducing the strength of regiments and relying on volunteers in their formation on the theory that a smaller provincial establishment composed of effectives was preferable to a larger one which existed only on paper.[18] Nevertheless, when Viceroy Bucareli assumed office he found that the provincials were still far from an effective fighting force and, therefore, undertook a second and more thorough reform.[19] This task was completed during his administration (1771–1779) and that of Martín de Mayorga (1779–1783), his successor. The strength of the army at the close of Mayorga's

administration is shown in Table 3, Appendix I. Despite the difficulties described and the conservative policy of Croix, the over-all result
of the successive reorganizations of the provincial militia was to
increase its table of organization strength from 9,244 to 16,755
(compare Tables 2 and 3, Appendix I).[20]

The reforms of the late Bourbons produced contingent consequences which in the long run were more important than the direct
achievements of the reforms themselves. Designed to strengthen the
empire, they ultimately contributed to its collapse. On the one hand,
they did not go far enough or take the right direction to remedy
the grievances of many Spanish Americans. On the other, their
"enlightened" and "liberal" character alienated influential sections
of the population. Perhaps most significant of all, they subverted
the order of a society which, with its hierarchical structure and
its emphasis on the traditional roles of church and crown, the several
social classes, and the various civic and economic corporations, was
almost medieval in character. Old institutions were affected both
absolutely and relatively. The expulsion of the Jesuits, for example,
and restrictions on the legal and economic privileges of the clergy
dictated by the regalism of Charles III weakened the authority and
prestige of the church. At the same time there were created new
groups, such as the army, whose structure cut across existing class
lines, and whose interests conflicted with each other and with established privilege and custom. Under strong and competent monarchs
these elements might have been reconciled and assimilated. Under
the weak successors of Charles, they contributed materially to the
turbulence and unrest which led to the disintegration of the empire.[21]

One of the most disturbing influences introduced into the society of
New Spain by the reforms of Charles III was the privileges of the
reorganized and expanded army. Among these the most important
was the *fuero privilegiado,* which conveyed the right to exercise or
to enjoy a jurisdiction independent of the *fuero real ordinario;* that
is, the royal or ordinary jurisdiction.[22] Such privileged *fueros* or
jurisdictions were the juridical expression of a society in which the
state was regarded not as a community of citizens enjoying equal
rights and responsibilities, but as a structure built of classes and
corporations, each with a unique and peculiar function to perform.[23]

Joaquín Escriche y Martín notes the existence of thirty-four privileged jurisdictions, which included those of the military, the clergy, the corporations of merchants, and the mining industry.[24] Each of these possessed its own tribunals which operated outside the hierarchy of royal courts.

A brief discussion of the background and structure of the privileged *fuero* of the army may be useful in appreciating its role in New Spain. In its most general form it was called the *fuero de guerra* and was first defined as a distinct legal code in two royal enactments promulgated respectively in 1551 and 1587. The first conceded military jurisdiction in civil and criminal causes to the officers and men of the companies of guards of the kingdoms of Castile, Navarre, and Granada. The second extended the same privilege to the entire military and naval establishment.[25] As the army expanded during the succeeding two centuries, and as it became necessary to define more precisely the relationship between it and other elements of society, the original concession was elaborated by royal enactment, court interpretation, and the accumulation of precedent. By the reign of Charles III the *fuero de guerra* constituted a large and complex body of law differentiated into several branches. The basic divisions were the *fuero de guerra militar*—generally shortened to the *fuero militar*—and the *fuero de guerra política*. The former pertained primarily to military personnel; the latter to civilian officials of the war and navy secretariats, the military finance department, and military hospitals.[26] The *fuero militar* was in turn subdivided into the *fuero militar privilegiado*—enjoyed by special corps such as the artillery, engineers, and provincial militia—and the *fuero militar ordinario,* which was conceded to the bulk of the army.[27]

In terms of its amplitude, the *fuero de guerra* varied according to the component of the army and the class of personnel affected. In some instances it extended to both civil and criminal actions. It was then classified as *íntegro* or *completo*. Where it was limited to criminal cases, it was called the *fuero criminal*.[28] Classified on another basis, it might be *pasivo* or *activo,* or both. The passive *fuero* affected the possessor only insofar as he was a defendant; that is, suits against him could be heard only by a tribunal of his particular jurisdiction. The active *fuero* conveyed to persons who enjoyed it the right to bring actions in their own tribunals against persons of another *fuero*. The active *fuero,* however, was the exception while the passive was the rule.[29]

Of the several subsidiary *fueros* deriving from the *fuero de guerra,* the most widely enjoyed, and hence the most important in the Spanish legal structure, were the *fuero militar ordinario* of the regular army and the *fuero militar privilegiado* of the militia. It is with these two that this study is concerned. The essential elements of the ordinary military *fuero* were codified in 1768 in a two-volume work entitled *Ordenanzas de S.M. para el régimen, disciplina, subordinación, y servicio de sus exércitos.*[30] By the terms of this code, the enjoyment of military jurisdiction in both civil and criminal causes was confirmed not only to officers and men of the regular army, but also to their wives and dependent children, their widows and surviving children during the latter's dependency, their domestic servants, and to certain civilian functionaries of the war department.[31] The ordinances are not explicit as to whether this *fuero* was active as well as passive. In practice, however, it appears to have been regarded as passive only, and this construction was confirmed in a royal decree of February 9, 1793.[32] Those who possessed the *fuero militar* also enjoyed military jurisdiction in the preparation of their wills and testaments and in the settlement of their estates.[33]

Although the military courts were thus granted a very broad competence, their authority was not absolute. In certain classes of cases considered to be particularly affected with the public interest, the ordinary courts retained jurisdiction. In others, competence might be granted to another privileged jurisdiction. Such exceptions were called cases of *desafuero*. Civil actions in this category included the disposition of entailed estates, litigation arising from debts and obligations incurred before entry into the service, suits for the recovery of usurped property, and actions in mercantile law. Criminal cases in which the soldier lost his *fuero* included those arising from offenses committed before entry into the service, malfeasance while holding public office, participation in public riots, sedition, gambling of a prohibited variety, disrespect or resistance to civil magistrates, violation of municipal police regulations, and frauds against the royal treasury.[34]

In addition to the *fuero militar,* officers and men of the regular army and their dependents enjoyed other privileges and immunities called *preeminencias.* They could not be called upon to assume municipal offices or discharge municipal responsibilities against their will; they were excepted from the charge of providing transportation, lodging, and subsistence for the army or for ecclesiastical and civil officials in transit except when these services were required for the direct use of the royal household; they were exempt from regular and special *servicios* (money aids to the crown); they could not be imprisoned for debt, nor could their arms, horses, or clothing be attached for such debts unless they were owed to the royal treasury. Moreover, officers and men who retired honorably from the service were entitled to *cédulas de preeminencias* which granted them for life the privileges just described and also the *fuero militar* to an extent which varied according to rank, length of service, and circumstances of retirement.[35]

The privileges of the Spanish militia varied according to the class concerned. In the instance of the provincials, the basic definition of their *fuero* was the *Ordenanza de milicias provinciales de España* issued in 1734. Various supplements and amendments to this act were issued from time to time, however, culminating in 1767 with the definitive *Real declaración sobre puntos esenciales de la Ordenanza de milicias provinciales de España.*[36] According to the provisions of the latter ordinance, when a provincial regiment was inactive, its officers and their wives and dependents enjoyed the complete *fuero militar* but enlisted men were conceded only the criminal *fuero.* When the unit was mobilized both officers and men with their wives and dependents possessed the complete *fuero.*[37] The declaration is not explicit as to whether the provincial *fuero* was active as well as passive.[38] In general it appears to have been passive only, although the active *fuero* might also be granted as a special concession, as was done in the instance of the officers and sergeants of the militia of Cuba and Yucatán.[39] Both officers and men and their wives were subject to military jurisdiction at all times in cases deriving from their wills and testaments.[40]

The provincials, like the regulars, were granted various *preeminencias.* They could not be compelled to hold municipal offices or dis-

charge municipal responsibilities; they were exempt from the charge
of providing quarters and subsistence for the regular army, and they
were relieved from a number of taxes and levies including regular
and special *servicios* and feudal dues. In situations where militiamen
were minors and thus were not subject to the charges and exactions
involved, the immunities and exemptions devolved upon their parents.
Upon honorable retirement officers and men were entitled to *cédulas
de preeminencias.* As was the case with the regulars, the privileges
conceded by these instruments varied according to rank, circumstances of retirement, and length of service.[41]

It is difficult to generalize about the privileges of the urban militia.
The *fuero* of the various units varied according to their location,
usefulness, and past services. In some instances officers and sergeants
enjoyed the complete *fuero militar,* while in others all personnel were
subject to the ordinary courts in all causes. Whenever urban units
were mobilized, however, they generally enjoyed the *fuero militar*
on the same terms as regulars.[42]

The machinery of the military jurisdiction differed according to
the particular *fuero* involved. For the regular army, the captains
general of the several military districts generally constituted the courts
of first instance for civil and testamentary cases and for criminal of-
fences which were not also military crimes.[43] In practice, such cases
were adjudicated by an *auditor de guerra* who was the trained legal
assistant of the captain general.[44] Appeals were to the *Consejo
Supremo de Guerra,* the highest military tribunal in Spain, and in
rare instances a final appeal could be made to the crown.[45] Cases
involving purely military offenses were tried by regimental courts-
martial *(consejos de guerra ordinarios)* when enlisted men were defendants and by courts-martial of general officers *(consejos de guerra
de oficiales generales)* when the charges were against officers.[46]

In regard to the militia, urban units, insofar as they enjoyed the
fuero militar, were subject to the same tribunals as the regular army.[47]
For the provincials, the court of primary jurisdiction was the colonel
of the regiment. This officer had a legal assistant who bore the
title of *asesor de guerra,* and who handled most of the proceedings
associated with the *fuero* of the provincials. Appeals followed the
same channels provided for other components of the army; that is,

to the *Consejo Supremo de Guerra* and thence to the crown.[48] In hearing suits which came under their jurisdiction, military tribunals of all classes, except for courts-martial, were governed by the same substantive and procedural law as was operative in the ordinary courts.[49]

As was the case with the main body of Spanish law, the *fuero militar* was transplanted to the overseas possessions, where initially primary and appellate jurisdiction over both regulars and militia was exercised by the colonial captains general, assisted as in Spain by *auditores* or *asesores*. Prior to the Seven Years' War, however, the military magistracy did not constitute a significant part of the legal structure of New Spain. Although the regular troops stationed in the viceroyalty enjoyed the same privileges as their European counterparts, their number was small.[50] In the case of the militia, the separate companies enjoyed a limited *fuero*. When not on active duty, enlisted men possessed neither the civil nor criminal *fuero*, and officers only the criminal, but when mobilized all ranks and grades enjoyed the same *fuero* as regulars.[51] In terms of the extent of the military jurisdiction these privileges amounted to little. At the time of Spain's entry into the Seven Years' War, the companies had not been mobilized for either training or active service for nearly twenty years,[52] and even the criminal *fuero* conceded to officers in peacetime was meaningless because most of the companies were defunct. When Viceroy the Marqués de Cruillas attempted to mobilize them in 1762 and 1763, he found that they had to be completely reformed and new officers commissioned.[53] Because of the limited services required of it, the urban militia of New Spain did not possess the *fuero militar* in any degree.[54]

The reorganization of the Army of New Spain begun by Villalba resulted in a significant increase of military privilege. Part of this expansion was represented by the increase in the regular army whose *fuero* and *preeminencias* were confirmed by a royal order of September 20, 1769.[55] A much more important extension of privilege occurred in connection with the provincial militia. In accordance with authorization contained in Villalba's instructions,[56] Viceroy Cruillas granted, on May 3, 1766, the newly organized regiments and battalions the same *fuero* enjoyed by the provincials of Spain; that is, civil and criminal actions against officers and criminal suits against enlisted men could be heard, except for cases of *desafuero*, only by the commanders of their regiments or separate battalions. When mobilized, all ranks and grades enjoyed the complete *fuero militar*. In addition, the provincials of New Spain were granted essentially the same *preeminencias* as their Spanish counterparts. The viceroy's declaration, however, specifically denied these amplified privileges to the old separate companies and also made an exception of the *pardos* enlisted in provincial units. The *pardos* were not to possess the *fuero militar* in any degree except when on active duty, but in the latter circumstance they enjoyed the same jurisdictional status as white provincials. On the other hand, as a special concession *pardos* were granted exemption during their period of service from the tribute to which they were ordinarily subject.[57] This levy amounted to two pesos and four *reales* annually for heads of families and half that amount for unmarried men.[58] When the provincial militia was reorganized by Bucareli, the *fuero* and *preeminencias* described above were incorporated into the regulations prepared for the several units.[59] On points not covered in the various declarations and regulations issued in New Spain, and in cases of doubts about their interpretation, the *Real declaración de milicias provinciales* was considered to apply.[60]

In addition to their qualitative amplification, the privileges of the militia of New Spain were extended in terms of the number of individuals who enjoyed them. Before 1765, this number was negligible, but as the militia establishment grew, the provincial *fuero* was extended to new units. Thus, by 1784, some 16,766 enlisted men possessed the criminal *fuero*, and some 639 officers the complete *fuero militar*.[61] More important than numbers alone, however, was distribution. Provincial units were raised not only in the communities whose names they bore but also throughout the provinces of which these communities were the administrative seats. For example, when Villalba formed the Regiment of Provincial Infantry of Toluca, Toluca itself furnished only one complete company and part of another. The remainder of the companies were raised in sixteen surrounding pueblos and haciendas.[62] Thus, the military jurisdiction was established in a large proportion of the provinces and communities of the viceroyalty. Moreover, many old and new companies which were not formally classified as provincial claimed the provincial *fuero* through broad construction of existing enactments or by special dispensation.

The most immediate and most obvious result of the expansion of military privilege was the appearance of numerous and sometimes prolonged and acrimonious disputes between the military magistracy on the one hand and the ordinary courts and other privileged tribunals on the other. Such conflicts were inevitable in a judicial structure characterized by a multiplicity of overlapping jurisdictions.[63] A soldier enjoying the military *fuero* was at the same time a vassal of the crown and was subject to the ordinary courts when his *fuero* was not complete and in cases of *desafuero*. As a communicant of the church, he was accountable for many of his actions to ordinary and extraordinary ecclesiastical judges. Moreover, he might also be engaged in some occupation which enjoyed a privileged *fuero,* and suits arising from pursuit of that occupation pertained to the cognizance of its special tribunals.

The crown tried to meet the problem of jurisdictional disputes, or *competencias* as they were called in legal terminology, in two ways. First, frequent enactments tried to define more precisely the boundaries between the several jurisdictions. The very number of such efforts, however, testifies to the difficulty and complexity of the problem.[64] Second, formulae were evolved for the settlement of disputes once they were initiated. In general, these provided that contending tribunals forward their cases through channels to their respective *consejos;* for example, to the *Consejo de Castilla* and the *Consejo Supremo de Guerra* in *competencias* involving, respectively, the ordinary and the military jurisdictions. The issue was then to be decided by consultations between representatives of the two bodies.[65] If, however, no accord could be reached, the case was appealed to a *junta de competencias* composed of impartial judges. In New Spain the faculty of arbitration resided in the viceroy.[66] While these procedures effected eventual settlement, they in no way held down the numbers of disputes.

Difficulties that were intrinsic in the Spanish judicial system were aggravated by the very human motivations of pride and jealousy, as well as of class- and self-interest. Soldiers placed a high value on their *fuero*, and they expected and sometimes got preferential treatment in their own tribunals.[67] Quite naturally, then, they claimed military jurisdiction at every opportunity whether or not their claims had a legal basis. Commanders tended to support the pretensions of their officers and men because they felt that the *fuero militar* constituted an incentive to enlistment and was an essential element in the maintenance of morale and *esprit de corps*.[68] The army, moreover, was very sensitive on points of "honor," and honor was intimately bound up with privilege. Consequently, it regarded with indignation attempts of civil officials to intervene in matters which affected its *fuero*. Civil magistrates, on their part, deplored military privilege as a subversion of their authority and prestige and resented the loss of fines and fees, upon which many of them depended, to military courts.[69] Their hostility was particularly pronounced in regions such as New Spain, where the *fuero militar* appeared to them as a pernicious innovation and a challenge to vested interests. Because of the strong feelings involved, extreme partisanship was not uncommon.[70]

In New Spain, the *fuero* of the militia was a much more serious problem than that of the regular army. In the first place, the militia was the most numerous and most widely distributed component of the military establishment. Second, militiamen, as civilians engaged in civilian pursuits, were much more likely to become parties to actions involving them in jurisdictional disputes than were regulars. Third, the organization of the militia was essentially local, and its officers and men, as only part-time soldiers, were in many instances subject to the jurisdiction of provincial civil magistrates—*alcaldes mayores* and *corregidores*—and local justices, the *alcaldes ordinarios*. At the same time, in the new provincial organization colonels and commanders, rather than the captain general, exercised primary military jurisdiction.[71] Thus, at the local and provincial level, the intimate contact of the ordinary and military magistracies provided constant opportunities for friction and rivalry. This situation may be contrasted with that of the regular army, which was to a large extent separated from civilian life both by its very nature and by the fact that at least half of it was stationed in isolated frontier garrisons. Moreover, jurisdiction over regulars in cases that were not purely military was exercised by the viceroy as captain general, an official who stood above local issues and rivalries.

Uncertainties about the nature and limits of the privileges of the militia complicated the situation. The declaration of Cruillas, limited in its application, was intended to serve only until a general ordinance could be prepared.[72] The latter project, however, was never consummated, and the militia continued to be governed by special declarations and unit regulations which were often provisional in character. The *Real declaración de milicias provinciales,* which was presumed to govern in cases of doubt, was not always adaptable to local circumstances such as, for example, the inclusion of the colored castes in many units. Moreover, rulings and interpretations regarding the various enactments in force in the viceroyalty varied according to the inclination of the several viceroys and their *auditores de guerra;* while the crown, itself, vacillated and procrastinated in resolving questions. Such an atmosphere provided an ideal breeding ground for controversies arising from both honest misunderstandings and partisan interests.

In the following chapters the history of the expansion of military privilege in New Spain will be treated in some detail, and a number of representative civil-military disputes will be analyzed. The evidence indicates that such disputes had an unfortunate effect on the administration of justice. In the first place, they consumed the time and attention of contending magistrates and of superior tribunals. Second, controversies were often protracted, and justice was delayed until they were settled. In criminal actions the guilty went unpunished and the innocent languished in prison; in civil suits delays resulted in loss and inconvenience to the interested parties. In addition to its effect on procedural aspects of justice, military privilege, or more properly its abuse, destroyed respect for law and order itself. The *fuero militar* was intended to convey to the military a jurisdiction which had definite limits and which would be exercised with responsibility. Instead, the army, and particularly the militia, regarded its *fuero* as absolute and, at the same time, as a general license for law evasion. This situation points to consequences which are difficult to document precisely but which are nonetheless evident. In Spanish tradition, jurisdiction was the essence of sovereignty, and to the vast majority of the population of New Spain, the local and provincial magistrates were the only visible representatives of royal jurisdiction. As the army grew and as these officials lost not only power but also prestige and respect, the very foundations of royal authority were undermined. This is a factor that has not been taken into account in explaining the disintegration of Spanish government in New Spain.

Finally, the privileges granted to the Army of New Spain were probably the most important factor in the creation of the praetorian tradition in Mexico. The *fuero militar,* along with honors and prestige associated with military service, was a fatal attraction to young creoles, and sons of the best families in New Spain sought commissions in regular and militia regiments. The ranks were filled from the lower classes to whom the *fuero* offered some measure of relief from their depressed status and an opportunity to evade the law. During the closing decades of Spanish dominion, the army, thus created, acquired prestige and power as the defender of the nation in the face of almost constant threats of war and invasion. By the very nature of its functions and constitution it was also a class apart and so regarded itself. The possession of special privileges enhanced its sense of uniqueness and superiority, and at the same time rendered it virtually immune from civil authority. Unfortunately, power and privilege were not accompanied by a commensurate sense of responsibility. A large proportion of officers and men regarded military service as an opportunity for the advancement of personal interests rather than as a civic obligation. Until the abdication of Ferdinand VII in 1808, the troublemaking potential of the military was held in check by a long tradition of loyalty to the crown. However, as the prestige of the monarchy declined in the following years, this limitation was removed and the army emerged as an autonomous and irresponsible institution. It was this army, under the banner of the Three Guarantees, that consummated independence and behind a façade of republican institutions made itself master of Mexico.

A Note on Citations

IN CITING MANUSCRIPT MATERIAL from the Archivo General de la
Nación, México, the abbreviation AGN is used. It is followed by a colon
and the designation of the particular *ramo* in which the material was
found, the volume within the *ramo*, and the number of the item, or *expediente*,
as it appears in the volume. The following abbreviations are employed for the
several *ramos*:

Bandos	B
Correspondencia de los Virreyes	CV
Historia	H
Impresas Oficiales	IO
Indiferente de Guerra	IG
Reales Cédulas	RC

To avoid unwieldy Roman numerals, Arabic figures are used for volume numbers. In the case of Correspondencia de los Virreyes the number of the volume
refers to its position within the subseries for each viceregal administration rather
than its numbered position within one of the three series which comprise the
ramo. It is believed that this practice will provide a more accurate reference
since there is some overlapping in the numbering of the three main series.
Thus: Croix to Arriaga, México, January 29, 1769, AGN:CV 13 (Croix),
no. 608. In citing items from Indiferente de Guerra, the volume number is
followed by the inclusive dates of the material it contains in order to differ-
entiate between volumes which sometimes carry the same number. Also, in
the volumes of the latter *ramo*, items are not numbered serially nor is there
generally any pagination. Therefore, in order to provide as precise a citation
as possible, items are followed by the title of the *expediente* in which they are
found. Thus: Juan Pérez Cano to Bucareli, México, October 13, 1773,
"Fuero Militar al Regim.ᵗᵒ de Milicias Urbanas de esta Ciudad," AGN:IG
47 (1773–1775).

Notes

(PAGES 1–2)

1. Herbert Ingram Priestley, *José de Gálvez, Visitor-General of New Spain,
(1765–1771)*, pp. 41–42.
2. Arthur S. Aiton, "Spanish Colonial Reorganization under the Family
Compact," *The Hispanic American Historical Review*, XII (August, 1932),
273–274.
3. *Ibid.*; Lillian Estelle Fisher, *The Intendant System in Spanish America*,
p. 8; Bailey W. Diffie, *Latin-American Civilization: Colonial Period*, pp. 421–
440, 574–575, 585–587, 625–629.
4. Félix Colón de Larriátegui, *Juzgados militares de España y sus Indias* . . . , II, pars. 824–843.
5. "Papel de puntos que ha tenido presentes el Virrey de Nueva España
. . . para fundar y asegurar . . . las defensas de estos preciosos Dominios,"

México, January 29, 1797, AGN:CV 4 (Branciforte, Reservada), no. 752, pars. 2–8; "Titulo de Theniente de la compania de Cavalleria Miliziana . . . del Pueblo de Cocupas . . . ," México, August 11, 1760, AGN:RC 119 (Duplicados).

6. Colón, II, pars. 1048–1104.

7. "Instrucción del sr. conde de Revillagigedo al sr. marqués de las Amarillas," México, November 28, 1754, *Instrucciones que los vireyes de Nueva España dejaron a sus sucesores* . . . , par. 133, p. 28.

8. "Estado de Revista . . . ," Guanajuato, November 8, 1767, AGN:IG 375 (1766–1767); *Informe* of the treasury officials of the Audiencia of New Galicia, Guadalajara, August 14, 1772, "Testim.º de los autos principales formados sobre averiguar el perjuicio, q.ᵉ se causa á la R.¹ Haz.ª en el Ramo de Tributos por el establecim.ᵗº de Milicias . . . ," AGN:IG 252 (1772). For the classification of the population of Spanish America on the basis of race and color, see Gonzalo Aguirre Beltrán, *La población negra de México, 1519–1810,* pp. 162–179, and Angel Rosenblat, *La población indígena de América desde 1492 hasta la actualidad,* pp. 263–293.

9. Aguirre Beltrán, p. 173; Rosenblat, p. 290, n. 7. Thus, in summarizing the results of the census of 1791–1792, Viceroy Revillagigedo divided the population of the viceroyalty, excluding Indians, into two classes; that is, *pardos* and persons of *casta limpia (Instrucción reservada que el conde de Revilla Gigedo, dió a su sucesor en el mando* . . . , pars. 579–580).

10. Aguirre Beltrán, pp. 165, 174–175, 273–275.

11. Aiton, 273–274; Royal instructions to Lieutenant General Juan de Villalba y Angulo, August 1, 1764, AGN:RC 85, no. 142, Introduction and par. 17 (cited hereinafter as Instructions to Villalba).

12. Viceroy the Marqués de Cruillas to Minister of the Indies Julián de Arriaga, México, January 2, 1765, AGN:CV 10 (Cruillas), no. 985.

13. The work of Villalba is treated more fully in Lyle N. McAlister, "The Reorganization of the Army of New Spain, 1763–1767," *The Hispanic American Historical Review,* XXXIII (February, 1953), 1–32.

14. Croix to Arriaga, México, March 25, 1767, AGN:CV 11 (Croix), no. 163; *id.* to *id.*, México, March 26, 1767, *ibid.,* no. 164; "La organización del ejército en Nueva España," *Boletín del archivo general de la nación,* XI (October–November–December, 1940), 633.

15. Royal order, January 5, 1768, AGN:RC 92, no. 9; royal order, February 7, 1771, AGN:RC 98, no. 32; Croix to Arriaga, México, June 18, 1768, AGN:CV 12 (Croix), no. 457.

16. The formation of new *fijo* units is treated in Chapter V.

17. "Notas que corresponden al Estado General . . . ," August 23, 1766, AGN:IG 236 (1766); Croix to Arriaga, México, October 27, 1766, AGN:CV 11 (Croix), no. 64; *id.* to *id.*, México, November 13, 1766, *ibid.,* no. 80; *id.* to *id.*, México, September 20, 1771, AGN:CV 14 (Croix), no. 1096.

18. Croix to Arriaga, México, September 23, 1766, AGN:CV 11 (Croix), no. 32; *id.* to *id.*, México, September 21, 1766, *ibid.,* no. 23; Croix to the Villa de Córdova, México, September 21, 1766, AGN:IG 151 (1765–1767); *id.* to *id.*, México, May 2, 1767, *ibid.*

19. Bucareli to Arriaga, México, October 5, 1771, AGN:CV 1 (Bucareli), no. 18; *id.* to *id.*, México, October 5, 1771, *ibid.,* no. 25; *id.* to *id.*, México, December 27, 1774, AGN:CV 45 (Bucareli), no. 1645.

20. For a fuller account of the growth of the Army of New Spain, see María del Carmen Velázquez, *El estado de guerra en Nueva España, 1760–1808.*

21. A stimulating discussion of the subversive effects of the Bourbon reforms

may be found in Cecil Jane, *Liberty and Despotism in Spanish America,* pp. 84 ff.

22. "Fuero," Joaquín Escriche y Martín, *Diccionario razonado de legislación y jurisprudencia* . . . , I, 822; "Fuero de guerra," *ibid.,* I, 1122.

23. Richard Konetzke, "Estado y sociedad en las Indias," *Estudios americanos,* III (January, 1951), 49.

24. "Jurisdicción especial o privilegiada," Escriche, II, 450–461.

25. Colón, I, lxxiii. More specifically, a royal decree of February 9, 1793, speaks of the "*fuero* and privileges conceded to military personnel by my august predecessors since the reigns of the kings Charles I and Philip II" ("Cumplim.ᵗᵒ a[1] R.¹ Decreto y orn acompañatoria . . . ," AGN:IG 13 [1792–1794]). Historically, the *fuero de guerra* had both medieval and Roman roots. During the reconquest Spanish warriors won various privileges and enjoyed a degree of extraordinary jurisdiction (Colón, I, lv-lxxiii). Indeed, the *fuero de hidalguía* derived from the fact that the first responsibility of the hidalgo was to bear arms in the service of his king, and it was in his capacity as a warrior that he was granted his privileges (*Novísima recopilación de las leyes de España,* Lib. VI, tít. ii, ley l, and tít. iv, ley 5; *Dictamen* of the *auditor de guerra,* México, December 16, 1773, "Fuero Militar al Regim.ᵗᵒ de Milicias Urbanas de esta Ciudad," AGN:IG 47 [1773–1775]). I am of the opinion, however, that more important than feudal precedent in determining the character of the *fuero de guerra* was the *magister militum;* that is, the extraordinary jurisdiction conceded to the Roman military tribunals by Emperor Constantine and confirmed and amplified by Justinian. A comparison of the Roman and the Spanish codes reveals a strong resemblance (see the comments of Colón, I, lxxi-lxxiii, xlvii-xlix and Juan de Solórzano y Pereira, *Política indiana* . . . , Lib. V, cap. xviii, núm. 6). Moreover, at the same time that a standing professional army was developing in Spain and the *fuero de guerra* emerged as a distinct code, Roman law dominated the thinking of Spanish jurists (John Thomas Vance, *The Background of Hispanic-American Law,* p. 118; John H. Parry, *The Audiencia of New Galicia in the Sixteenth Century,* pp. 2–3). It would seem reasonable to assume, therefore, that Roman precedent strongly influenced military as well as civil jurisprudence.

26. "Fuero de guerra," Escriche, I, 1122.

27. "Jurisdicción militar," *ibid.,* II, 456.

28. José Vicente y Caravantes, *Tratado de procedimientos en los juzgados militares* . . . , Primera parte, tít. i, par. 2.

29. *Ibid.,* Primera parte, tít. i, par. 4; "Fuero activo y pasivo," Escriche, I, 831.

30. Cited hereinafter as *Ordenanzas de S.M.*

31. *Ordenanzas de S.M.,* Trat. VIII, tít. i, arts. 1–2, 5, 8–9.

32. The articles of the *Ordenanzas de S.M.* cited in the note immediately above merely confirm the concession of the *fuero militar* to the personnel of the regular army without specifying whether it was active as well as passive. However, the *Recopilación de leyes de los reinos de las Indias,* in speaking of the *fuero* of regular troops in the overseas possessions, states that military magistrates will take cognizance of the causes of military personnel when the latter are defendants (Lib. III, tít. xi, ley 1). This interpretation was repeated in the instructions given to the Marqués de las Amarillas upon his appointment as viceroy of New Spain ("Instrucción general que trajó de la corte el marqués de las Amarillas . . . ," Aranjuez, May 17, 1755, *Instrucciones que los vireyes de Nueva España dejaron a sus sucesores,* par. 40, p. 72). The royal decree of February 9, 1793, uses the words: ". . . military

magistrates will have in the future private and exclusive cognizance of all cases, civil and criminal, which are brought against personnel of my army. . . ." (Cumplim.^{to} a[1] R.^{1} Decreto y o̅r̅n̅ acompañatoria. . . ."). See also "Jurisdicción militar," Escriche, II, 457.

33. *Ordenanzas de S.M.*, Trat. VIII, tít. xi, arts. 1–5.

34. *Ibid.*, Trat. VIII, tít. ii; Vicente, Primera parte, tít. ii, pars. 24–25.

35. *Ordenanzas de S.M.*, Trat. VIII, tít. i, arts. 3–4, 6–7; Colón, I, pars. 8–13. The laws governing the nature and extent of the *fuero* and *preeminencias* of the regular army in the last decade of the eighteenth century were codified and subjected to an extensive commentary in the previously cited work of Colón de Larriátegui. The more important provisions of the ordinances of 1768 and of later additions and amendments may be found in the *Novísima recopilación*, Lib. VI, tít. iv. A more recent compilation of the military code is the previously cited *Tratado* of Vicente y Caravantes, while the *Diccionario* of Escriche y Martín provides an easy reference for information on the military jurisdiction.

36. *Novísima recopilación*, Lib. VI, tít. iv., leyes 7–10; Colón, II, pars. 828–840. The declaration of 1767 will be cited hereinafter as *Real declaración de milicias provinciales*.

37. *Real declaración de milicias provinciales*, Tít. VII, arts. 12, 26–27, 29, 37–39, and Tít. VIII, art. 16.

38. The definitive articles merely state (1), that officers shall enjoy the same *fuero* and *preeminencias* as the regular army, and (2), that all members of the provincial militia will enjoy the criminal *fuero* while the regiment is inactive, but that when it is mobilized they and their wives will possess the *fuero militar* on the same terms as regulars (Tít. VII, arts. 12, 29). In neither case is it specified whether this *fuero* is passive only or both active and passive.

39. *Reglamento para las milicias de infantería de la provincia de Yucatán, y Campeche . . .* , Tít. XI, art. 5; "Fuero de guerra," José María Zamora y Coronado, *Biblioteca de legislación ultramarina . . .* , III, 325–326.

40. *Real declaración de milicias provinciales*, Tít. VII, art. 8.

41. *Ibid.*, Tít. VII, arts. 1–4, 9–15, 32–36; Colón, II, pars. 857–888.

42. Colón, II, pars. 1049–1104.

43. *Ordenanzas de S.M.*, Trat. VIII, tít. iv, art. 1, and tít. xi, art. 5; Vicente, Primera parte, tít. v, par. 222. There were some exceptions to this rule. For example, in permanent military posts and forts, the military governors possessed original jurisdiction (*ibid.*, pars. 269–275).

44. *Ordenanzas de S.M.*, Trat. VIII, tít. iv, art. 1 and tít. viii, art. 1; Vicente, Primera parte, tít. v, pars. 222, 231–233, 236.

45. *Ordenanzas de S.M.*, Trat. VIII, tít. iv, art. 3. The *Consejo Supremo de Guerra* was formed of senior military and naval officers plus a representation of civilian legal and clerical personnel. In addition to its function as a high court of appeals, it concerned itself with matters of top-level military policy and administration (Vicente, Primera parte, tít. v, pars. 149–152; Gaston Desdevises du Dezert, "Les institutions de l'Espagne au XVIIIe siècle," *Revue hispanique, LXX* (June-August, 1927), 126–128.

46. *Ordenanzas de S.M.*, Trat. VIII, tít. v, art. 1, and tít. vi, art. i.

47. Colón, II, par. 1049.

48. *Real declaración de milicias provinciales*, Tít. VIII, arts. 16–18.

49. *Ibid.*, Tít. VIII, art. 16; Colón, II, par. 908.

50. *Recopilación de Indias*, Lib. III, tít. xi, leyes 1–2; Solórzano, Lib. V, cap. xviii, núms. 6–7; Revillagigedo, *Instrucción reservada*, par. 98. In certain

cases final appeals to the *Junta de Guerra de Indias,* a special chamber of the Council of the Indies, were allowed (Louis G. Kahle, "The Spanish Colonial Judiciary," *The Southwestern Social Science Quarterly,* XXXII [June, 1951], 36; Solórzano, Lib. V, cap. xviii, núms. 11–12). After the military reforms of Charles III, apparently such appeals went to the *Consejo Supremo de Guerra* (Colón, II, par. 290).

51. *Recopilación de Indias,* Lib. III, tít. xi, leyes 1–2; *Dictamen* of the *auditor,* México, February 3, 1764, AGN:IG 57.

52. "Expedientes sobre organizacion de milicias . . . ," AGN:IG 213 (1758–1760).

53. Cruillas to Arriaga, México, March 19, 1763, AGN:CV 10 (Cruillas), no. 935.

54. The Regiment of Commerce certainly did not enjoy the *fuero militar (Informe* of Inspector General Francisco Antonio Crespo, México, December 22, 1784, "Expediente sobre incidente entre el Real Tribunal del Consulado y el Regimiento del Comercio de Mexico," AGN:IG 122 [1783–1894 *(sic)*], pars. 4, 138 [cited hereinafter as Crespo, "Informe"]). It is probable, therefore, that neither did the other urban units of New Spain.

55. Colón, par. 287. This order declared that the *Ordenanzas de S.M.* had full force and authority in the Indies.

56. Instructions to Villalba, par. 36.

57. *Bando,* AGN:IO 6, fol. 77.

58. Fabián de Fonseca and Carlos de Urrutía, *Historia general de real hacienda . . . ,* I, pars. 20–22, pp. 418–419.

59. For example, the "Reglamento Provicional de Milicias de Villa de Córdoba y Xalapa," México, January 14, 1775, AGN:IG 51 (1773–1775), Cap. VI. This regulation is reproduced in "El ejército de Nueva España a fines del siglo XVIII," *Boletín del archivo general de la nación,* IX (April-May-June, 1938), 240–269.

60. I have found no enactment extending the peninsular declaration to New Spain. However, officials of the viceroyalty appear to have considered it in force (Croix to Arriaga, México, June 28, 1771, AGN:CV 14 [Croix], no. 1033; Croix to the Captain General of New Galicia, México, July 28, 1770, "Testim.° del Quad.ⁿᵒ de autos formados sobre Testamentos de los Militares . . . ," AGN:IG 252 [1772]; Croix to the Audiencia of New Galicia, México, February 19, 1771, *ibid.*).

61. The figure for enlisted militiamen enjoying the criminal *fuero* is the same as the total strength of the provincial militia shown in Table 3, Appendix I, because as indicated in note 1 to the table, this strength probably represents the total number of enlisted provincials but does not include officers or regular cadres. The number of provincial officers enjoying the complete *fuero militar* was determined by totalling the officer strength of units classified as provincial. Unit totals were derived from tables of organization when available and when not by applying a normal officer-enlisted man ratio. Figures for both officers and enlisted men, however, are only approximations. On the one hand they are based on the assumption that all units subsisted at full strength, which was generally not the case. On the other, they do not include various urban and miscellaneous units which claimed the *fuero* of provincials but whose jurisdictional status was uncertain.

62. *Estado* of the Regiment of Toluca, December 9, 1765, AGN:RC 88, no. 77.

63. See the comments of Colón, I, lxx, lxxvi-lxxvii, and Revillagigedo, *Instrucción reservada,* pars. 117–119. For an excellent modern study of the

judicial structure in the Spanish American colonies see Ricardo Zorraquín Becú, *La organización judicial argentina en el periodo hispánico.*

64. In the *Ordenanzas de S.M.,* for example, the *fuero* of the regular army is redefined and clarified in order to "halt the [disputes] which arise from claims to the possession of the *fuero militar* by many who ought not to enjoy it and the subjection to other tribunals, through ignorance, of persons to whom it is conceded. . . ." (Trat. **VIII**, tít. i, art. 1). Twenty-five years later, the previously cited royal decree of February 9, 1793, again seeks to define the *fuero militar* to prevent the ". . . grave injuries to the State and the discipline of my troops because of the disputes which so frequently arise between the military and other jurisdictions ("Cumplim.ᵗᵒ a[1] R.¹ Decreto y orn acompañatoria. . . . ").

65. *Novísima recopilación,* Lib. IV, tít. i, ley 15, and notes 4–15 to ley 15.

66. Revillagigedo, *Instrucción reservada,* par. 93.

67. See the comments in *ibid.,* par. 118.

68. That this attitude existed at the highest level of command may be indicated by again citing the royal decree of February 9, 1793, whose preamble reads:

The considerable understrength suffered by the army for many years made it necessary to draft 12,000 men from the militia in 1770, and to institute general levies in 1773, 1775, and 1776, to fill the vacancies. This situation can be attributed, according to the reports of various senior officers and the representations of my *Consejo Supremo de Guerra,* to the contraction, in many cases, of the *fuero* and privileges conceded to military personnel by my august predecessors since the reigns of the kings Charles I and Philip II (Cumplim.ᵗᵒ a[1] R.¹ Decreto y orn acompañatoria. . . .").

See also the comments of Colón, I, xi-xii, xxxiv-xxxviii, II, par. 834, and Antonio Xavier Pérez y López, *Teatro de la legislación universal de España é Indias . . . ,* XX, 160–161.

69. John H. Parry, *The Sale of Public Office in the Spanish Indies . . . ,* pp. 7–9, 24–25.

70. Colón, I, lxxvii.

71. "Reglamento Provicional de Milicias de Villa de Córdoba y Xalapa," Cap. VII, art. 12.

72. Instructions to Villalba, par. 48.

TWO

The Military and the Ordinary Jurisdiction

THE REORGANIZATION of the militia begun by General Villalba was not extended immediately to the Pacific provinces of New Spain where the old separate companies continued to exist. These, it will be recalled, were excluded from the enjoyment of the amplified privileges conceded by Viceroy Cruillas to the provincials. Nevertheless, in December, 1767, Diego Garabito, commandant of the armed forces of New Galicia, issued a directive to militia commanders granting to the companies of the province the same *fuero* and *preeminencias* defined in the viceroy's declaration. The authority for this action is not stated, but Garabito justified it on the ground that the privileges of the militia must be thoroughly understood by commanders so that they could defend their men against the "aggressions" of civil magistrates. Cases of such aggression, said the commandant, had resulted in a noticeable deterioration of morale among militiamen.[1]* It is not clear who was to exercise military jurisdiction under the terms of the directive, since the units affected were not organized into regiments and battalions with their colonels and lieutenant colonels. Apparently competence in the first instance pertained to commandants of groups of companies, with appeals going to the senior *oidor* of the Audiencia of New Galicia, who functioned as captain general in cases involving the militia.[2]

Garabito's directive was not welcomed by the civil magistrates. In July, 1768, Mariano Pérez y Alamillo, *alcalde mayor* of Purificación and Tomatlán, dispatched a complaint to the audiencia. The commandant's action, Pérez admitted, may have been inspired by his zeal for the service, but it did not take into account the character and circumstances of the inhabitants of the province. For the most part they were ignorant and illiterate and had no understanding of legal principles and procedures. Specifically, those enlisted in the militia could not grasp the nature and extent of the privileges and

*Chapter notes are on page 30.

22

responsibilities conveyed by the *fuero militar*. As a result, there were "daily" disturbances and disputes between militiamen and the royal justices, and the respect due to the latter was seriously undermined. Ignorance, he continued, was compounded by deliberate abuse of military privilege by militia officers. Most of the population of his jurisdiction, including personnel of the militia, engaged in some type of trade. Thus, the officers became involved in business transactions with civilians or with their own men. In these dealings, the *alcalde mayor* charged, the civilians and enlisted men were often defrauded because officers not only claimed the *fuero militar* in their transactions but were also the local representatives of the military jurisdiction. Thus they could divert or dispose of actions against themselves, and the injured parties were too poor to appeal to the captain general.[3]

Two months later Pérez directed a more specific protest to the audiencia. On the order of Garabito, he reported, the captain of the company of militia of Tomatlán had sequestered the hacienda of Diego Salaises, deceased corporal of the same company, and had refused to allow him to proceed with the inventory of the estate. Pérez refused to recognize the authority of Garabito's order and petitioned the audiencia to confirm his competence in the case.[4]

The audiencia took no immediate action on the first and more general complaint of Pérez, but it requested Garabito to show authority for his order in the case of the hacienda of Salaises.[5] In response, the commandant cited a royal decree of March 25, 1752, which confirmed the competence of military tribunals in the disposition of estates of deceased army personnel.[6] The decree, however, spoke only of soldiers who died "teniendo salario," that is, on active status, a wording which apparently excluded the militia. Anticipating a challenge on this point, Garabito quoted a circular order issued in 1759 by the *Consejo Supremo de Guerra,* which stated that to obviate any doubts and disputes that might arise from the terminology of the decree of 1752, the latter was interpreted to apply to the militia as well as the regular army.[7] The commandant added that in view of these dispositions he was at a loss to understand the reluctance of Pérez to recognize the competence of the militia jurisdiction.[8]

Upon the receipt of Garabito's reply, the audiencia remitted it to the *fiscal*, Arangoyti, for an opinion. The latter's comments con-

stituted a direct rebuttal of the commandant's arguments. As Garabito had foreseen, they were based on the fact that the decree of 1752
apparently did not apply to the militia. In regard to the order of
the *Consejo Supremo de Guerra* cited by the commandant, the *fiscal*
pointed out that the Laws of the Indies ordered colonial officials
to honor—but suspend—*(obedescan, y no cumplan)* enactments of
the royal councils of Spain unless they were endorsed and forwarded
via the Council of the Indies.[9] Since the order in question had not
received this endorsement, it was not in force in New Spain. Arangoyti's statement concluded with the request that the commandant
be informed of the provisions of the Laws of the Indies so that in
the future he might abstain from citing irrelevant legislation to
support his actions.[10]

The audiencia, as might be expected of a representative of the
ordinary jurisdiction, inclined toward the argument of the *fiscal*
and recommended to the captain general that the competence of
the ordinary justices be upheld in the disposition of the estates of
deceased militiamen.[11] The captain general agreed with the audiencia
and accordingly ordered that Garabito's directive be suspended insofar as it applied to testamentary actions. To resolve any doubts
that might remain, however, he asked Viceroy Croix for a definitive
decision.[12]

Croix's answer was brief and explicit, consisting merely of a direct
quotation from artículo 8, Tratado VII, of the *Real declaración de
milicias provinciales,* which stated that the provincial militia enjoyed
military jurisdiction in the disposition of estates on the same terms
as those conceded to regulars in the decree of 1752.[13] It should be
added that probably neither of the contending parties was familiar
with the royal declaration, which was promulgated on May 30, 1767,
although copies did not reach New Spain until June, 1770—and then
in insufficient quantities for general distribution.[14] In resolving the
issue, Croix seems to have disregarded the distinction between the
old and the new militia established in Cruillas' *bando* of May 3,
1766, and, in effect, to have raised the companies of New Galicia
to provincial status. Despite the categorical nature of Croix's declaration, the audiencia was not willing to concede. Although it ordered
the justices of the province to recognize the competence of the

military jurisdiction in testamentary actions, it proposed to renew the *competencia*. Accordingly, it requested the *fiscal* to suggest a line of action.[15]

In the meantime, a dispute between local civil and military officials had developed over another aspect of jurisdiction. Early in March, 1770, Manuel Benites, a sergeant of militia, appeared in the court of Josef Montes de Oca, lieutenant in Ahuacatlán of the *alcalde mayor* of Ahuacatlán and Jala, seeking satisfaction for injuries allegedly sustained by two of his burros at the hands of Lázaro Silbestre, an Indian of Jala. Upon investigating the complaint, the justice assessed Silbestre thirteen pesos damages, but the latter claimed that he could raise only eleven pesos. Montes accepted this sum as a settlement. When, however, Benites called at the residence of the justice to collect his damages and was informed of the amount of the settlement, he became highly indignant.[16] Without dismounting from his horse or removing his hat in respect for the office held by Montes, he proceeded to denounce the latter in loud and violent terms for perverting justice. When Montes requested him to moderate his language, he refused and continued his tirade. The justice thereupon ordered him under arrest in the house of Josef de Ynda, an ensign in the local militia, but Benites resisted on the grounds that the ordinary jurisdiction had no authority to arrest him and that he owed obedience only to his immediate superior, Ensign Ynda. During the altercation a crowd gathered to witness, as Montes put it, the "humiliation of a royal justice."[17]

Shortly thereafter, the captain of Benites' company, Juan de la Rosa y Casanovo, was informed of the incident by Ynda. Rosa immediately wrote to Montes stating that while he deplored the excesses of Benites, the sergeant enjoyed the *fuero militar* in criminal actions in which he became involved as a defendant. The affront to the civil justice fell in this category. The captain requested, therefore, that the culprit and the evidence against him be turned over to his jurisdiction and promised that if guilty the sergeant would receive appropriate punishment.[18]

The actual disposition of Benites at this point in the dispute is not clear. The *Real declaración de milicias provinciales* granted to the ordinary justices the power to arrest personnel of the militia.

They were, however, required to notify the nearest officer or non-commissioned officer of the arrest on the same day and to provide the appropriate militia magistrate with a copy of the charges within twenty-four hours. If jurisdiction pertained to the latter, the prisoner was to be remanded to his custody. If the offense was a case of *desafuero,* the arresting authority retained custody.[19] Resistance to arrest was such a case and competence should have pertained to the ordinary jurisdiction.[20] As indicated above, however, the disputants do not appear to have been familiar with the royal declaration, nor if they had been is it likely that either the letter or the spirit of the law would have taken precedence over questions of pride and prestige. What appears to have happened is that Benites eventually accepted arrest by Ensign Ynda and remained at least informally in military custody, because a few days after the incident Montes charged that Ynda had allowed the sergeant to break arrest and that the latter was going about his business openly. In any case, Montes ordered the records of the case sent to Commandant Garabito with a request for a decision as to whether competence belonged to the military or to the ordinary jurisdiction.[21]

On this occasion Garabito displayed a most cooperative attitude. In his reply he castigated the militia officers of the province of Ahuacatlán and Jala for their incompetence and particularly for their failure to instruct their men in the limits of their *fuero.* To remedy the situation and to prevent repetitions of incidents such as the one precipitated by Benites, the commandant provisionally conceded jurisdiction to Montes in all actions, civil and criminal, involving the militia of his district. Garabito also promised to order the commanders of the companies affected to respect Montes' competence.[22]

Garabito's efforts toward conciliation, however, did not achieve the desired result, and some three months later the dispute was revived. On June 28, 1770, Juan Antonio Brin de Támez, who apparently succeeded Montes as lieutenant of justice in Ahuacatlán, observed Raymundo Sabalza, later identified as a militiaman, enter a private residence carrying a knife long enough to classify it as a prohibited weapon. Brin approached Sabalza with the purpose of depriving him of the knife and placing him under arrest for violation of police ordinances. The offender, however, not only refused to recognize

Brin's authority but drew the blade and threatened to use it against the magistrate. Brin shouted for help, and Antonio de Esquivel, another militiaman, appeared on the scene. Sabalza thereupon picked up several stones from the street with the evident purpose of throwing them at the justice and Esquivel. The latter quickly withdrew. Brin then abandoned his attempts to arrest Sabalza personally but sent a message to Ensign Ynda seeking aid from the militia. Ynda, however, when he discovered that Sabalza was a militiaman, refused to cooperate with the civil justice and insisted on taking the culprit into military custody. Thus the ordinary jurisdiction was again flouted and, to make matters worse, when Brin attempted to accumulate testimony on the case, he discovered that Ensign Ynda had forbidden all militiamen to testify. Brin sent a report of the case to Bartholomé Flores de Abrego, *alcalde mayor* of Ahuacatlán and Jala, along with a statement that many other incidents of a similar nature had occurred in his district, but that he was not forwarding accounts of them because of the difficulty of obtaining evidence from militiamen.[23]

The experience of his two lieutenants prompted Flores to dispatch to the audiencia summaries of the cases involving Benites and Sabalza and of the action of Ynda in prohibiting his men from testifying. The evidence was accompanied by a strongly worded protest against what Flores termed encroachments on the royal jurisdiction. The *alcalde mayor* charged that as a consequence of the incidents cited, and of the refusal of the military authorities to punish miscreants, militiamen were encouraged to commit excesses and were openly contemptuous of royal magistrates. In his province, Flores continued, nearly all the adult male inhabitants were enlisted in the militia. He therefore found himself without the authority or prestige necessary to administer justice. The *alcalde mayor* blamed this unfortunate situation on the directive of Garabito which conceded the provincial *fuero* to the militia of New Galicia. Flores concluded by petitioning the audiencia to issue a statement of policy supporting the authority of the ordinary jurisdiction and to use its power to see that all those who defied or insulted royal justices were properly punished.[24]

As a result of Flores' complaints, the *abogado fiscal* of the audiencia prepared on September 13, 1770, a formal statement on the controversy with the military. In regard to the legal aspects of the dispute over testamentary jurisdiction, he merely recapitulated the arguments offered by Arangoyti in the case of the hacienda of Salaises. There were, however, practical features of the question that he felt should be considered. Most important of these was the fact that the principal source of income for the provincial justices was the fees they collected for the inventory and division of estates. Generalizing on the statement of Flores, the *fiscal* asserted that the militiamen constituted the bulk of the male population in districts where companies existed, and warned that if the disposition of their estates were to be removed from the competence of the ordinary jurisdiction, the justices would be unable to maintain themselves and their families or to meet the expenses of their offices. Under these circumstances, he said, it would be difficult to find responsible persons to occupy the offices of *alcalde mayor* and *corregidor*. Moreover, if anyone should accept such an office, he would be obliged to support himself by extortion from those subjects who were not fortunate enough to be enrolled in the militia.[25]

The *fiscal* next expressed himself on the more general problems raised by the concession of the *fuero* of provincials to the companies of New Galicia. Seconding Flores, he asserted that militiamen considered themselves entirely free from subordination to royal justices and regarded the *fuero militar* as a cloak behind which all manner of wrongdoing could be concealed. The lawlessness and insolence of the enlisted men, he continued, was overlooked or even abetted by their officers. That this situation existed was evidenced by the testimony of the *alcalde mayor* of Ahuacatlán and Jala, which could be supported by citing many other instances of disrespect for royal justices that had occurred throughout the realm.

The *fiscal* also seized the opportunity to launch a general attack on the militia organization of New Galicia. Not only had it produced positive damages to the administration of justice, but it served no useful function. The reasons for raising companies in the first place were to provide protection against the raids of barbarous Indians and to preserve internal security. Since the former danger had largely disappeared, and since the docility and loyalty of the population precluded any domestic disturbance, the original reasons were no longer valid. The *fiscal* was confident, moreover, that in the event of a threat of invasion by some hostile European power the people would spring to arms to defend their homes and their religion without the need for an elaborate military organization prior to the event. The *fiscal* concluded his opinion by recommending to the audiencia that testimony from the *expedientes* originating in Tomatlán and Ahuacatlán be forwarded to the viceroy, along with a plea that the privileges of the militia of New Galicia be abrogated or at least limited so that the orderly administration of justice could be restored.[26]

The audiencia found itself in substantial agreement with the *fiscal*. In December of 1770, it requested Viceroy Croix to reverse his decision regarding competence in testamentary actions on the ground that he had not had all the evidence or the full arguments of the audiencia at his disposal in making it. He was also asked to issue appropriate orders to prevent abuses of the *fuero militar* by the militia.[27] As before, Croix's answer was brief and to the point. In regard to testamentary jurisdiction, he remarked rather caustically that in making his original decision he had been thoroughly familiar with the audiencia's case. That decision still stood. Remedies for cases of disrespect to royal justices, he continued, could be found in the *Real declaración de milicias provinciales* and in other pertinent enactments. Furthermore, he suggested that both civil and military authorities might do well to familiarize themselves with military ordinances instead of engaging in unproductive controversies and in molesting the viceroy.[28] Again, however, the audiencia was unwilling to acknowledge defeat and in March, 1771, it ordered the entire question reappealed, this time to the crown.[29] In the fullness of time its persistence was rewarded. Some ten years later a royal order denied the *fuero militar* in civil, criminal, and testamentary actions to the militia of New Galicia except when it was mobilized for active service.[30] Thus, in effect, the companies were established as urban rather than provincial, but the triumph of the ordinary jurisdiction was short-lived. As will be shown later, new circumstances soon led to a reopening and an expansion of the controversy.

Notes

1. *Instrucción* of Garabito, Guadalajara, December 22, 1767, "Testim.° del Quad.ⁿᵒ de autos formados sobre Testamentos de los Militares . . . ," AGN:IG 252 (1772).
2. I base this conclusion on a study of the handling of several cases. On the duties of the senior *oidor* of the audiencia as captain general see Captain General of New Galicia to Croix, Guadalajara, December 20, 1768, *ibid.*
3. *Consulta* of Pérez, Purificación, July 14, 1768, *ibid.*
4. *Consulta* of Pérez, Purificación, September 7, 1768, *ibid.*
5. *Auto,* Guadalajara, September 18, 1768, *ibid.*
6. Garabito to the audiencia, Guadalajara, September 18, 1768, *ibid.*
7. For a summary of enactments dealing with the competence of military tribunals in the disposition of estates, see Zamora, VI, 26 ff.
8. Garabito to the audiencia, Guadalajara, September 18, 1768, "Testim.° del Quad.ⁿᵒ de autos formados. . . ."
9. *Recopilación de Indias,* Lib. II, tít. i, leyes 39, 40.
10. *Pedimento* of the *fiscal,* Guadalajara, September 30, 1768, and *Dictamen* of the *fiscal,* Guadalajara, [1768], "Testim.° del Quad.ⁿᵒ de autos formados. . . ."   11. *Auto,* Guadalajara, November 5, 1768, *ibid.*
12. Captain General of New Galicia to Croix, Guadalajara, December 20, 1768, *ibid.*
13. Croix to Captain General of New Galicia, México, July 28, 1770, *ibid.*
14. Croix to Arriaga, México, June 2, 1770, AGN:CV 13 (Croix), no. 888.
15. *Auto,* Guadalajara, August 7, 1770, "Testim.° del Quad.ⁿᵒ de autos formados. . . ."
16. Testimony of Montes, Ahuacatlán, March 13, 1770, *ibid.* The source of his indignation is not made clear by the testimony. He was apparently either dissatisfied with the original damages assessed or with the reduction accepted by Montes.   17. *Ibid.*
18. Ixtlán, March 14, 1770, *ibid.*   19. Trat. VIII, arts. 20–21.
20. *Ordenanzas de S.M.,* Trat. VIII, tít. ii, art. 1.
21. Decree, Ahuacatlán, March 24, 1770, "Testim.° del Quad.ⁿᵒ de autos formados. . . ."
22. Garabito to Montes, Guadalajara, March 30, 1770, *ibid.*
23. Testimony of Brin, Ahuacatlán, June 30, 1770, *ibid.*
24. *Consulta* of Flores, Ixtlán, July 3, 1770, *ibid.*
25. "Testim.° del Quad.ⁿᵒ de autos formados. . . ." For a more authoritative statement on the poverty of the provincial justices and the resulting temptation to engage in extortion and illicit activities see "Instrucción del sr. conde de Revillagigedo al sr. marqués de las Amarillas," México, November 28, 1754, *"Instrucciones que los vireyes de Nueva España dejaron a sus sucesores,* pars. 36–37, p. 12.
26. *Representación* of the *abogado fiscal,* Guadalajara, September 13, 1770, "Testim.° del Quad.ⁿᵒ de autos formados. . . ."
27. *Auto,* Guadalajara, October 11, 1770, *ibid.;* Croix to the Audiencia of New Galicia, México, February 19, 1771, *ibid.*
28. Croix to the Audiencia of New Galicia, México, February 19, 1771, *ibid.*
29. *Auto,* Guadalajara, March 20, 1771, *ibid.*
30. Royal order, October 29, 1781, summarized in Eusebio Bentura Beleña, *Recopilación sumaria de todos los autos acordados de la real audiencia y sala del crimen de esta Nueva España . . . ,* I, 343.

THREE

The Military and the Mercantile Jurisdiction

ALTHOUGH the military magistracy had as its principal opponent the ordinary jurisdiction, it also clashed with other privileged *fueros*. One of the most protracted and acrimonious disputes in this category involved the Regiment of Commerce of Mexico and the Tribunal of the Consulado of Mexico. The Regiment of Commerce, it will be remembered, was of the urban class and prior to Villalba's mission had not possessed the *fuero militar* in any degree. Moreover, it did not benefit by virtue of Cruillas' concession because it was obviously not among the new provincial units formed in 1765 and 1766. Shortly after Cruillas' declaration, however, the colonel of the regiment, the Marqués de Rivas Cacho, petitioned the viceroy to extend the *fuero* of the provincial militia to his command. Such a move was essential, he claimed, to satisfy the clamors of his officers and men and to uphold the honor and prestige of the regiment.[1]*

No immediate action was taken on the request, possibly because of the press of business incident to the replacement of Viceroy Cruillas by the Marqués de Croix. Soon after the installation of the new viceroy, however, Juan Pérez Cano, who succeeded Rivas Cacho in command of the regiment, renewed the petition. At the same time, the commanders of the urban cavalry companies of the capital asked that the provincial *fuero* be conceded to their units.[2] Croix was inclined to be sympathetic to these requests. During the first years of his administration he was haunted by fears of an English invasion or of a domestic uprising abetted by the English.[3] If an emergency should arise, the urban militia of the capital would have to be mobilized to guard public installations and maintain order. He felt, therefore, that the concession of the *fuero* to them was necessary to stimulate their enthusiasm for the military service.[4] When, however, the concession was made in September, 1767, the order mentioned only the cavalry units.[5]

*Chapter notes begin on page 40.

The reason for the omission of the Regiment of Commerce is not clear. The members of that unit, however, interpreted the concession as applying to themselves, and Croix apparently intended that it should.[6] On the other hand, both civil and military magistrates entertained doubts about the *fuero* of the regiment. In July, 1771, the *fiscal* of the Audiencia of Mexico requested that the question be settled by formally granting the infantry unit the same privileges that were enjoyed by the urban cavalry.[7] In January of the following year, the *auditor de guerra* stated that he needed a clarification of the jurisdictional status of the officers and men of the regiment in order to process cases in which they became involved.[8] Viceroy Bucareli responded to these representations by declaring that the Regiment of Commerce should be understood as included in Croix's concession of the *fuero* to the urban cavalry and that both units should enjoy the same privileges as provincials.[9] This enactment was confirmed by a royal order of January 20, 1773.[10]

Bucareli's action created a more serious problem than the one it was designed to solve. In effect his declaration meant that civil and criminal actions against officers of the regiment and criminal suits against enlisted men could, with the exception of cases of *desafuero,* be heard in the first instance only by the colonel in his capacity as military magistrate. However, the same officers and men were presumed to be engaged in commerce, and actions arising from contractual arrangements between merchants—and among merchants and partners, associates, factors, agents, insurers, and carriers—pertained to the mercantile jurisdiction. In New Spain this was exercised in the first instance by the Tribunal of the Consulado of Mexico, which consisted of a prior and two consuls. Appeals went to a *juzgado de alzadas,* a special appeals court, composed of an *oidor* of the Audiencia of Mexico and two members of the merchant community.[11] The crown had attempted to define the boundary between the two *fueros* by confirming the competence of mercantile courts in commercial actions and by specifically prohibiting jurisdiction to the military magistracy in such cases.[12] After the confirmation of their *fuero,* however, the members of the Regiment of Commerce, vigorously supported by their colonel, disregarded the prohibition and strove to extend their privileges at the expense of the consulado.

Inasmuch as the officers and men of the regiment were ostensibly merchants enrolled in the consulado and were soldiers by avocation only, some explanation of their attitude is in order. Part of the answer lay in their conviction that they would be treated more leniently under military jurisdiction than in the Tribunal of the Consulado. Another factor was a metamorphosis that took place in the character of the personnel of the unit. In practice the more substantial merchants tended to avoid personal service, and many of them enlisted their employees in their stead.[13] Moreover, after Villalba's reorganization of the militia many traders of scant means who wished to avoid more rigorous service in the provincials and at the same time enjoy military privileges were allowed to enlist in the regiment even though they were not members of the merchant guild. Inspector General Francisco Crespo complained that in order to acquire the status of *tratante* and become eligible for enlistment, "it was sufficient for any poor man to put up a stall in the Plaza or the Baratillo and stock it with a bag of chile which he sells a few pods at a time, or with a few pieces of worthless iron or three or four worn volumes of romances or comedies."[14]

The change in the constitution of the regiment was accelerated when, in 1781, the regular garrison of the capital was withdrawn to defend Veracruz against a possible English invasion and the commercial unit was mobilized.[15] The active status of the regiment further discouraged the more substantial members of the consulado from serving personally. Moreover, they were reluctant to spare their employees for extended periods. They therefore adopted the practice of hiring substitutes—*alquilones*, as they were called—from the lowest and most irresponsible elements of the population.[16] Even in the instance of the officer corps, the majority of the posts were held by individuals who were not members of the merchant guild.[17] In referring to the situation, the consulado complained that most of the officers sought commissions not because of their devotion to the king's service but in order to obtain the annual subsidies paid to them by the merchant guild for the upkeep of their units.[18] Thus the regiment, instead of being an organization of merchants who voluntarily devoted their time and resources to military training, acquired a distinctly mercenary complexion.[19] A large proportion of both officers and

men gave their first loyalty to the regiment rather than to the
consulado. They regarded the efforts of the merchant guild to
exercise its authority as an invasion of their military privileges and,
in some cases at least, as a threat to their private interests.[20]

An example may illustrate their attitude. In 1773 Roque Varela,
an officer of the regiment, was arrested for debt on the demand of
a Spanish merchant. In view of the fact that the case involved two
members of the merchant community, it appears that competence
certainly should have pertained to the Tribunal of the Consulado.
Varela, however, claimed military jurisdiction on the grounds of
his *fuero militar* and was supported by Colonel Pérez. This claim
was denied by the arresting officer and a *competencia* was formed
and submitted to the viceroy for resolution. On the basis of the
prohibition placed on the military jurisdiction in mercantile matters,
the *auditor de guerra* confirmed the competence of the mercantile
tribunal and Bucareli issued an order to that effect. The colonel
protested the decision vociferously. It revoked, he contended, the
concessions made by Croix and by Bucareli himself; it constituted
a clear case of discrimination against the regiment; and it struck a
serious blow against the morale of his officers and men. His pro-
tests, however, did not convince the viceroy and the decision stood.[21]

Despite its setback in the Varela case, the Regiment of Commerce
continued to exploit its *fuero*. In April, 1782, Francisco Velasco, a
soldier of the regiment, was arrested at the instance of the Tribunal
of the Consulado and confined in the public jail of the capital.
Colonel Pérez demanded that the prisoner be remanded to military
custody and proposed to confine him in the guardhouse which had
been established when the regiment was mobilized in 1781. The
mercantile tribunal, however, refused to comply. Pérez' demand
was strongly supported by Inspector General Pascual de Cisneros,
who took a strict view of his responsibilities as defender of the privileges of the militia.[22] Being unable to reach an agreement, the parties
appealed to higher authority.[23] Although initially the *auditor de
guerra* supported the position of the consulado,[24] the regiment
managed to keep the dispute open. For the next two years, two
successive viceroys, Martín de Mayorga and Matías de Gálvez,
were harassed by representations growing increasingly acrimonious,

as the disputants presented their views on the proper place of confinement for members of the regiment.

The case of the military faction rested on two principal arguments, the first of which was emotional. Colonel Pérez, apparently somewhat chastened by the decision in the case of Roque Varela, did not challenge the competence of the Tribunal of the Consulado in mercantile actions. He claimed, however, that it was humiliating for members of his command who were, as he put it, "nobles honrados y [de] distinción por la sola qualidad de Soldados" to be incarcerated with "gente de la más baxa extracción." Their morale, he warned, would be destroyed by the knowledge that such treatment was to be their reward for their sacrifices. Moreover, the spectacle of his troops languishing in a public prison dimmed the luster and compromised the honor of the regiment. Pérez went on to assert that these injuries could be avoided if, when his men had to be arrested by civil authorities, they were kept in military custody. He offered the assurance that they would be as well guarded and as equally at the disposition of the consulado as if they were in the public jail.[25]

The second argument, which was advanced by Inspector General Cisneros, attempted to justify military custody on legal grounds. His reasoning is rather difficult to follow. On the one hand he conceded, as had Pérez, the competence of the consulado in cases such as the one involving Velasco, but contended that the jurisdiction of the mercantile tribunal would in no way be limited by confining the prisoner in the guardhouse pending the hearing of the case. On the other he argued that regulations provided that when a soldier was arrested by a civil magistrate and a dispute over competence arose, the prisoner should remain in military custody until the dispute was decided.[26] Therefore, the consulado was violating the *fuero* of Velasco by holding him in the public jail. By the latter argument he seems to have implied that there was some doubt about jurisdiction in Velasco's case after all, thereby contradicting his initial acknowledgment of the competence of the merchant tribunal.[27]

The consulado based its case largely on a refutation of the arguments of Pérez and Cisneros. It termed the colonel's apprehension for the honor of his regiment ridiculous and contended that there was no question of honor involved in the dispute. Jails were jails, it asserted flatly, and confinement in one was neither more nor less humiliating than in another. Does a civilian, it queried, who is remanded to military custody for complicity in desertion acquire honor by being confined in a military guardhouse?[28] In regard to the complaint of Cisneros that the regiment's *fuero* was being violated, and the assurance of the inspector general and the colonel that prisoners were just as much at the disposition of the mercantile tribunal in the regimental guardhouse as in the public jail, the consulado felt that the position of the military arose from ignorance of the true meaning of the words *fuero* and *competencia*. The essence of any *fuero*, it maintained, was jurisdiction. About the jurisdiction of the Tribunal of the Consulado in Velasco's case and in commercial cases in general there was no doubt; this had been admitted by both the colonel and the inspector general. Therefore, the argument of Cisneros that soldiers should remain in military custody until competence was decided was irrelevant since that question had already been resolved and there was no *competencia*. Moreover, continued the consulado, jurisdiction was a broader concept than the inspector general realized. It involved the entire judicial process from the arrest of the defendant through the final disposition of the case and, more specifically, included confinement. Although a prisoner arrested in the guardhouse might conceivably be at the disposition of, or available to, the merchant court, the law provided that he should be under the authority of the magistrate having jurisdiction.[29] This would not be the case if he were in military custody. Since the Tribunal of the Consulado customarily employed the public jail for the confinement of its prisoners, that was the place for Velasco and others like him. Instead of abridging his *fuero* by leaving him there, the mercantile *fuero* would be violated by placing him in the guardhouse.[30]

The consulado also had something to say about Pérez' assurance that prisoners were well guarded in the regimental guardhouse. Such a statement, it asserted, was not born out by its experience. Two cases were cited where members of the regiment had been arrested for debt and, at the request of the colonel, had been remanded to military custody. In both instances, it was charged, the prisoners were allowed to come and go freely and to converse with their family and associates. Such neglect was prejudicial to commerce because it allowed the debtors to dispose of their assets surreptitiously to the detriment of their creditors. The members of the regiment themselves, continued the consulado, had a poor opinion of the security of the guardhouse; when they instituted suits against one of their comrades for debt, they insisted that the defendant be confined in the public jail where he could be securely guarded.[31]

When, in anticipation of the retirement of the regiment from active duty, Inspector General Cisneros recommended the retention of the guardhouse as a permanent establishment, the consulado again expressed itself on the subject. The dispute over confinement, it charged, was promoted by a sinister cabal of officers and men of bad character whose actions were not only offensive to the merchant guild but also injurious to public order. Some employed counterfeit pesos and false measures in their business in violation of the authority of the *fiel ejecutoría,* a municipal agency charged with the enforcement of enactments regulating retail trade in the interest of the consuming public.[32] Others sold prohibited beverages, an offense which came under the jurisdiction of a special court, the *Juzgado de Bebidas Prohibidas.*[33] Still others acted as pawnbrokers for the poor and hungry without complying with municipal police regulations. The consulado maintained that these individuals claimed the *fuero militar* to avoid punishment. They preferred the guardhouse to the public jail because in the former, despite the good intentions of the colonel, they enjoyed a degree of freedom that would not be tolerated in the latter. Furthermore, the lax discipline that prevailed in the guardhouse encouraged the prisoners to indulge in gambling and other vices offensive in the eyes of God. The consulado petitioned, therefore, that the viceroy not only abolish the guardhouse at once but also impose perpetual silence on those who were pressing for its permanent establishment.[34]

The dispute was eventually decided by Viceroy Matías de Gálvez in a decree of March 18, 1784, which in the strongest terms supported the position of the consulado. The controversy was blamed entirely on the efforts of the regiment to extend its privileges in a manner contrary to the intent of the crown and prejudicial to the administration of justice and the public welfare. The jurisdiction of the Tribunal of the Consulado in mercantile actions involving members of the regiment was categorically confirmed, and the viceroy prescribed that this jurisdiction continued even when the unit was on active status. Moreover, there was to be no further argument about the matter. Officers and men of the regiment were enjoined to cease their exaggerated claims and to accept the consular jurisdiction without resistance and in good faith. In regard to the specific question involved in the dispute, Gálvez confirmed the authority of the consulado to confine regimental personnel in the public jail and ordered that the regimental guardhouse be closed permanently. Further representations on the subject from the military faction were forbidden. Finally, apparently as a result of the consulado's charges, the decree confirmed jurisdiction over members of the regiment to the ordinary courts in cases involving violation of municipal police ordinances; to the *Juzgado de Bebidas Prohibidas* in cases arising from the manufacture and sale of prohibited beverages; and to the *fiel ejecutoría* where the charge was the use of false weights, measures, or money.[35]

Although the regiment felt very much put upon by Gálvez' decision and appealed to the crown for a vindication of its "honor," events were at work which were to deal it an even more severe setback.[36] At about the same time that it was quarreling with the consulado over the confinement of its members, the *fuero* of the company of pork-butchers of Mexico produced a prolonged controversy. In 1781, Manuel Ximénez de Arenal contracted with Fernando Antonio Landero to take over the management of two butcher-shops which belonged to the former. At the time these establishments were being operated by Baltasar Fernández Liger, a soldier in the company, who desired to terminate his contract with Ximénez. When the time came, however, for the delivery of the two shops to the new manager, Fernández objected to certain terms of the transfer. The difficulty was eventually composed, but in the process Fernández cursed and insulted Landero. In order to vindicate his honor, the latter lodged charges against Fernández before the senior *alcalde ordinario* of the capital. This magistrate arrested Fernández. But the accused denied the jurisdiction of the *alcalde* on the ground that he possessed the *fuero militar*, and a *competencia* was formed. In his decision, Viceroy Mayorga declared that Fernández' denial was justified and that his case pertained to the military courts.

Landero appealed to the crown (apparently because he did not get satisfaction in the military courts, or because he feared he would not get it). On August 2, 1784, a royal cedula reversed the viceroy's decision and ordered the action returned to the ordinary jurisdiction. The cedula further declared that there was no documentary evidence that the *fuero militar* had ever been granted to the company of pork-butchers. The action of the crown, however, did not terminate the dispute. The *auditor de guerra* of Mexico pointed out that by virtue of the declaration made by Croix on September 9, 1767 (which the crown had apparently overlooked), the company enjoyed the provincial *fuero*. The question was, therefore, whether the cedula just cited or the declaration of Croix ruled in the case of Fernández and in other actions involving the members of the company. To obtain an answer, the regent captain general appealed to the crown.[37]

Disputes over the *fuero* of the urban militia were not limited to Mexico City. In 1785, the lieutenant of the governor of Yucatán wrote to the Audiencia of Mexico:

The claims of the several tribunals in matters of jurisdiction and of individuals regarding their privileged *fueros,* daily promote doubts and *competencias* which are as delicate to deal with as they are destructive to public harmony and, not a few times, to the just settlement which the nature and importance of the cases demands. Therefore, there is no matter of greater importance that could be brought to the attention of higher authority, and I petition Your Highness to publish the true *fuero militar* which the urban militia ought to enjoy in time of peace.[38]

The accumulation of complaints and queries, such as those discussed in the preceding pages, induced the crown to take summary action. On February 13, 1786, it declared that, on the basis of the precedent established for New Galicia, the urban militia of the Indies possessed the *fuero militar* only when on active duty.[39] Thus the source of dispute between the Regiment of Commerce and the Consulado of Mexico was removed. The settlement, however, was only temporary. As will be shown later, the question of the *fuero* of the regiment arose again and was argued just as vigorously during the administrations of viceroys Revillagigedo and the Marqués de Branciforte.

Notes

1. Juan Pérez Cano to Bucareli, México, October 13, 1773, "Fuero Militar al Regim.ᵗᵒ de Milicias Urbanas de esta Ciudad," AGN:IG 47 (1773–1775).
2. *Bando*, México, September 9, 1767, *ibid.;* Croix to Arriaga, September 23, 1766, AGN:CV 11 (Croix), no. 27.
3. Croix to Arriaga, México, September 26, 1766, AGN:CV 11 (Croix), no. 40; *id.* to *id.,* México, January 26, 1767, *ibid.,* no. 119.
4. *Bando*, México, September 9, 1767, "Fuero Militar al Regim.ᵗᵒ de Milicias Urbanas. . . ."; Croix to Arriaga, México, September 23, 1766, AGN:CV 11 (Croix), no. 27.
5. *Bando*, México, September 9, 1767, "Fuero Militar al Regim.ᵗᵒ de Milicias Urbanas. . . ."
6. Pérez to Bucareli, México, October 13, 1773, *ibid.;* Croix to Arriaga, México, September 23, 1766, AGN:CV 11 (Croix), no. 27.
7. Pérez to Bucareli, México, October 13, 1773, "Fuero Militar al Regim.ᵗᵒ de Milicias Urbanas. . . ."
8. Domingo Valcarcel to Bucareli, México, January 10, 1772, *ibid.*
9. Decree, México, February 17, 1772, *ibid.*
10. AGN:RC 102, no. 9.
11. *Recopilación de Indias,* Lib. IX, tít. xxxxvi, leyes 28, 37–38. A brief modern treatment of the judicial functions of the tribunal is contained in Robert S. Smith, "The Institution of the Consulado in New Spain," *The Hispanic American Historical Review,* XXIV (February, 1944), 64–67, 78, while a fuller account of the character, origins, and development of the mercantile jurisdiction may be found in the same author's *The Spanish Guild Merchant. A History of the Consulado, 1250–1700,* Chapter II.
12. *Ordenanzas de S.M.,* Trat. VIII, tít. ii, art. 4.
13. Pérez to the king, México, February 20, 1786, "Expediente sobre incidente entre el Real Tribunal del Consulado y el Regimiento del Comercio de Mexico," AGN:IG 122 (1783–1894 [*sic*.]); Crespo, "Informe," par. 66; Consulado to Revillagigedo, México, October 24, 1791, "Sobre dar nueba forma al Regimiento Urbano del Comercio de Mexico," AGN:IG 122 (1783–1894 [*sic*]).
14. Crespo, "Informe," par. 68.
15. Mayorga to Minister of the Indies José de Gálvez, México, July 29, 1781, AGN:CV 8 (Mayorga), no. 1184.
16. Pérez to the king, México, February 20, 1786, "Expediente sobre incidente. . . ."; Crespo, "Informe," pars. 66–67, 71–75. The practice of using *alquilones,* it might be added, served to extend the *fuero militar,* since this privilege was claimed by both the hirelings and the merchants whose place they took ("Dictamen del Coronel D.ⁿ Fran.ᶜᵒ Antonio Crespo, Inspector interino de las tropas del Virreynato de N.ᵃ Esp.ᵃ sobre su mejor arreglo y extablecim.ᵗᵒ," México, July 31, 1784, Biblioteca Nacional de México, MS. 173, par. 303. Cited hereinafter as Crespo, "Dictamen").
17. Crespo reported that in 1784, twenty-four of the thirty-seven officers on the rolls were not members of the consulado (Crespo to the viceroy [1784], "Expediente sobre incidente. . . .").
18. Consulado to Matías de Gálvez, México, September 1, 1783, *ibid.*
19. Hipólito Villarroel in his very critical analysis of Mexicans and their institutions wrote of the regiment: "But it is also clear that the majority are mercenary soldiers, hired men clothed in military equipment and uniforms who

perform military service only as long as their wages are paid by the respective captains of companies. Afterwards, they become vagabonds and idlers and are a heavy charge upon the public" *(México por dentro y fuera bajo el gobierno de los vireyes,* p. 171).

20. In the words of the consulado, ". . . miran al Cuerpo [the regiment] como Padrastros, quando el Consulado le atiende como legitimo Padre. . . ." (Consulado to Matías de Gálvez, México, December 17, 1783, "Expediente sobre incidente. . . .").

21. Pérez to Bucareli, México, October 13, 1773, and *Dictamen* of the *auditor,* México, December 16, 1773, "Fuero Militar al Regim.ᵗᵒ de Milicias Urbanas. . . ."

22. The *Real declaración de milicias provinciales* provided that the Inspector General of Militia was *juez privativo* and commandant general of that component in all matters pertaining to its formation, administration, discipline, training, finance, and preservation of its privileges (Tít. X, art. 8).

23. Pérez to Mayorga, México, June 19, 1782, and Cisneros to Mayorga, México, April 25, 1782, "Expediente sobre incidente. . . ."

24. *Dictamen* of the *auditor,* México, May 31, 1782, *ibid.*

25. Pérez to Mayorga, México, June 19, 1782, *ibid.*

26. This argument was apparently based on the *Real declaración de milicias provinciales,* Trat. VIII, art. 21, which could be so construed.

27. Cisneros to Mayorga, México, April 25, 1782, "Expediente sobre incidente. . . ."; Cisneros to Matías de Gálvez, México, June 20, 1783, *ibid.*; *Dictamen of* Cisneros, México, June 20, 1783, *ibid.*

28. Civilians became subject to the military jurisdiction when they were charged with certain offenses which were considered to affect particularly the army. Among these was complicity in desertion *(Ordenanzas de S.M.,* Trat. VIII, tít. ii, arts. 1–5).

29. The law cited was possibly Tít. VIII, art. 21, of the *Real declaración de milicias provinciales,* which could be so construed.

30. Consulado to Matías de Gálvez, México, July 12, 1782, and *id.* to *id.,* México, December 17, 1783, "Expediente sobre incidente. . . ."

31. *Id.* to *id.,* México, July 12, 1782, *ibid.*

32. The specific functions of the *fiel ejecutoría* varied somewhat from community to community but generally included supervision of weights and measures and the establishment and enforcement of just prices and standards of quality. Its authority included not only inspection but also the citation, trial, and sentencing of violators ("Fieles ejecutores," Zamora, III, 247–251; Constantino Bayle, *Los cabildos seculares en la América española,* Primera parte, ch. X).

33. The *Juzgado de Bebidas Prohibidas,* as its title suggests, was concerned with violations of prohibitions against the manufacture and sale of certain beverages such as, for example, *chinguirito,* a low-grade rum. In New Spain it was united to the *Tribunal de la Acordada,* a special criminal court which dealt with crimes of violence (Fernando Casado Fernández-Mensaque, "El Tribunal de la Acordada de Nueva España," *Anuario de estudios americanos,* VII [1950], 279–323).

34. Consulado to Matías de Gálvez, México, September 1, 1783, and *id.* to *id.,* December 17, 1783, "Expediente sobre incidente. . . ."

35. "Expediente sobre incidente. . . ."

36. "Exped.ᵗᵉ a representaz.ⁿ de los ofiz.ˡᵉˢ del com.ᵒ de Mexico s̄r̄ē q.ᵉ se de cuenta al Rey con la q.ᵉ acompañan para vindicar el honor del cuerpo," May, 1786, AGN:IG 122 (1783–1894 [*sic*]).

37. Regent to Minister of the Indies José de Gálvez, México, April 24, 1785, AGN:CV 1 (Royal Audiencia), no. 377.

38. "Consulta del Ten.ᵗᵉ de Gov.ᵒʳ de la Prov.ᵃ de Yucatan sobre el fuero q.ᵉ deben gozar aquellas milicias en t̄p̄o de Paz," Mérida, June 8, 1785, AGN:IG 394 (1778–1787).

39. AGN:RC 133, no. 95.

FOUR

The Privileges of the Pardos

THE ROLE to be played by the *pardos* in the armed forces of New Spain was a source of concern to both civil and military officials. In the opinion of their social superiors, the colored castes were irresponsible, lazy, vice-ridden, and politically unreliable, "la gente más peor y vil" of colonial society.[1]* Because of their alleged moral deficiencies they were excluded by law from regular units.[2] They were, however, more inclined to military service than were whites and also displayed a superior resistance to the climate and diseases of tropical stations. It was found expedient, therefore, to admit them into regular garrisons as early as the first half of the sixteenth century.[3] *Pardos* also had to be used in forming the old militia companies in Mexico, along the Gulf and Pacific coasts, and in other parts of the viceroyalty where they constituted a significant part of the population.[4]

After the military reorganization of the 1760's the enlistment of *pardos* in regular units was continued, but only with the misgivings and even the opposition of many commanders who feared that they would transmit their vices to Spanish soldiers with whom they served.[5] General Villalba was authorized to use his discretion regarding the admission of the colored castes into the reformed militia. If he used them, he was directed to take into consideration the prejudices of the whites in deciding whether to incorporate them into mixed units or organize them separately.[6] Villalba chose the latter alternative and reorganized the existing colored companies of Mexico and Puebla into provincial battalions. As the militia program expanded, *pardos* were used extensively in districts where there were not enough whites to raise the required number of men. During the administration of Viceroy Croix, new colored units were formed and old ones reorganized in Veracruz, Córdova, Jalapa, San Luis Potosí, Guanajuato, and Oaxaca. In addition, many companies of *pardos* that had been raised before Villalba's mission remained in existence.[7]

*Chapter notes begin on page 51.

It will be recalled that Viceroy Cruillas' declaration of the *fuero* of the provincial militia specifically excluded the *pardos*. Croix, however, feared that such discrimination would discourage their participation in the militia program, and on December 24, 1767, he granted to them the same *fuero* which the white provincials enjoyed.[8] This concession created new opportunities for controversy. In the first place, it failed to distinguish between the new provincial units and the miscellaneous separate companies whose jurisdictional status was in doubt. Thus the question of which *pardos* enjoyed the *fuero militar* was left open. Moreover, civil magistrates regarded the possession of this privilege by the *pardos* with particular abhorrence. Immunity from the ordinary jurisdiction, they feared, would encourage the lawlessness and licentiousness to which the colored castes were addicted by nature and would ameliorate the inferior social and civic status imposed on them by law. As a consequence the established order of society would be subverted.[9] It might be added that a number of military men, such as viceroys Bucareli and Revillagigedo, who also had responsibilities as civil administrators, shared this attitude.[10]

A special source of concern to civil officials was the exemption from tribute conceded to *pardos* enlisted in the provincial militia. This privilege resulted in a diminution of the revenues of the *ramo de tributos* and was prejudicial to the interests of the royal treasury. Actually the loss was not large, and in any one year probably did not exceed 12,500 pesos.[11] This figure is not impressive when compared to an average annual tribute collection of 788,261 pesos for the period 1770–1780, and 840,918 for the following decade.[12] It is even less so when measured against the total annual revenue of the treasury, which during the period 1756–1770 averaged well over 6,000,000 pesos, and which by 1802 reached 20,000,000.[13] The exemption question, however, derived more from broader considerations of policy than from the relatively small sum involved. The state of the royal treasury was a peculiarly sensitive point in Spanish colonial administration. Colonial governments were under standing orders to spare no effort to augment public revenues and to tolerate only those expenses and reductions in income which were essential to the maintenance of good government.[14] Moreover, the merit of administrators was to a large extent judged on their success in achieving these objectives.[15]

During the last four decades of the eighteenth century, pressure on colonial officials tended to increase. The almost continuous wars and rumors of war which distracted Spain during that period required heavy expenditures for defense, and the overseas treasuries were expected to bear a large share of the burden. In appointing José de Gálvez as visitor-general of New Spain in 1765, the king cited as a reason, "the large sums needed in attending to the obligations of my royal crown," and the necessity "to exhaust all means which mav appear conducive to increasing as much as possible the income of the revenues." Gálvez was directed to "regulate the system and management with which the revenues are to be administered in [the] future, reducing expenses and salaries which can and ought to be lowered or abolished, so that the balances be not dissipated by unnecessary expense, but made more effective to their destined ends."[16] The state of the *ramo de tributos,* it might be added, was of particular concern to the visitor-general because in the late 1760's collections had fallen off sharply as a result of epidemics and the failure of authorities to register many tributaries who lived in the larger cities.[17]

Because of the considerations outlined above, treasury officials deplored even the small loss occasioned by the exemption of the *pardos.* Their concern was shared by the audiencias which also had fiscal responsibilities and which, in any case, were no friends of military privilege.[18] Viceroys found that their responsibilities as superintendents of the royal treasury conflicted with their duties, as captains general, to maintain the militia at maximum strength.[19] Furthermore, the exemption caused great inconvenience to *alcaldes mayores, corregidores,* and their lieutenants, who were directly responsible for the collection of tribute. These functionaries were required to deliver fixed annual amounts based on tribute rolls prepared every three to five years.[20] If, in the middle of such a period, tributaries were enlisted in the militia, some means had to be devised to compensate for the loss until the next revision of the rolls.

The problems raised by the exemption of *pardo* militiamen from tribute were complicated, as in the case of their *fuero,* by widespread doubts as to just which units enjoyed the privilege. Initially, exemption had been granted only to the provincial units raised by Villalba or, more specifically, the battalions of Mexico and Puebla. Subsequently, however, the companies organized or reorganized by Croix and many of the old units which had not been reformed claimed the privilege either on the basis of a broad construction of Cruillas' original declaration or by virtue of earlier special grants.[21] In order to dispel the uncertainty, Visitor-General José de Gálvez proposed to Croix that as a general policy only those *pardos* enlisted in units formally classified as provincial should enjoy exemption. Thus, the pretensions of the various separate companies scattered throughout the viceroyalty would be disposed of. In 1771 Croix circulated a declaration incorporating Gálvez' proposal to the *contador de tributos* and to the Audiencia of Mexico. For reasons not explained, copies were not distributed to militia commanders or to provincial officials. In order to remedy the omission, the visitor-general recommended to Viceroy Bucareli, who succeeded Croix, that the decision be published by *bando* throughout the viceroyalty.[22] The new viceroy expressed himself as concerned and ordered a thorough investigation of the question. He did not see fit, however, to act on Gálvez' proposal.[23] The reason for his hesitancy is not clear. In view of the fact that he hoped to reorganize the militia, it is possible that he felt the program should be completed and the number and kind of units fixed before any general statement of their privileges be made. In any case the uncertainty continued throughout his administration.

The hostility of civil officials toward the exemption of *pardo* militiamen, the value which the *pardos* themselves placed on this privilege, and the uncertainty regarding when and where it should be enjoyed, together constituted a source of constant friction and controversy. The problem may be illustrated by following the course of a dispute that developed in New Galicia where most of the militia was drawn from the colored castes.[24] In 1771 Commandant Diego Garabito, in compliance with the orders of Viceroy Croix, instructed the justices to recruit the militia companies of their districts to a strength of eighty men.[25] In issuing these instructions, Garabito stressed that tributaries should be used only when absolutely necessary. Late in the same year, however, Agapito Martínez, justice of Santa María

del Oro [Tequepespan], reported that to comply with the commandant's directive he had found it necessary to enlist eighty *pardos*.
Martínez, therefore, requested that the collections due from him
according to the tribute list for the current five-year period be
reduced by the amount lost through the enlistment of the eighty
tributaries.[26] Some months later the *corregidor* of Tequila petitioned
the Audiencia of New Galicia for a similar reduction on the
grounds that he had had to enlist twenty-five tributaries in order to
fill the company of *pardos* established in his district.[27]

Despite objections from the treasury officials and the *fiscal*, the
audiencia ruled that the commutations be granted.[28] The two peti-
tions, however, directed its attention to a situation which might do
substantial harm to the treasury, and therefore it decided to make a
general inquiry into the participation of the tributary *pardos* in the
militia program of the province. This investigation developed along
two lines. First, Commandant Garabito was requested, through the
captain general, to submit a report showing the number of companies
of militia that existed in the jurisdiction of Tequila, the authority for
their existence, and his warrant for maintaining their strength at
eighty men.[29] In compliance, the commandant presented rosters
of the companies of *pardos* of Tequila, Ixtlán, and Ahuacatlán. The
authorization for their formation, he asserted, was a viceregal order
issued in 1762 which directed a general reorganization of the militia
of New Galicia. Thereafter, the perfection of their organization was
an integral part of his responsibilities as commandant-in-chief. In
regard to their strength, Garabito maintained that this was the footing
prescribed by the general military ordinances of 1768.[30]

Garabito's statement was channeled to the *fiscal*, Arangoyti, for
comments and recommendations. That official was most willing to
express himself. Indeed, he appears to have regarded the tribute
question as a ready-made opportunity to renew the controversy
which had begun over the question of the *fuero* of the militia.
The *fiscal* conceded that authority for the establishment of militia in
New Galicia existed, but pointed out that the order cited by Garabito
had prescribed that companies be formed on a footing of fifty men.
Despite this limitation, he continued, in many cases the justices had
formed larger units and, furthermore, more companies had been

raised than were really necessary for defense. This mistake, the *fiscal* charged, had been compounded by formally increasing the strength of companies to eighty men. As to the authority cited by Garabito for the latter step, Arangoyti argued that the general military ordinances were designed for the needs of the regular army of Spain and not for the militia of the colonies. Moreover, it was well known that the laws of Castile had no force in New Galicia if they conflicted with viceregal enactments affecting the latter province.

The *fiscal* then turned to the heart of the issue. Before the reorganization of the Army of New Spain, he asserted, and before the attendant amplification of military privilege, it would have made little difference if all the men in New Galicia were enrolled in the militia. Now, however, the immunity of militiamen from the jurisdiction of the ordinary justices led to constant disputes and miscarriages of justice. At the same time their exemption from tribute resulted in a diminution of the revenues of the royal treasury. In concluding his opinion, the *fiscal* recommended that a protest against the unnecessary and unauthorized inflation of the militia and of the resultant evils be sent to the viceroy.[31]

As its second line of inquiry, the audiencia asked the treasury officials to report the total number of tributary *pardos* in the militia and the annual loss to the treasury resulting from their exemption. It also requested recommendations for measures which would remedy the loss, but which at the same time would not jeopardize the security of the realm.[32] Three months later the treasury officials submitted their findings. In the eleven provinces where militia existed, they reported, there were forty-one companies totalling 2,859 men. Twenty-four of the companies were made up of *pardos* and had a total strength of 1,807; the remaining seventeen companies were composed of whites. Of the *pardos*, 1,205 were full tributaries and, at the rate of two-and-a-half pesos each, would pay 3,012 pesos, 4 *tomines* annually in tribute if it were not for their exemption. The remaining 602 *pardos* were half-tributaries and, at the rate of one-and-one-quarter pesos, would normally pay 752 pesos, 4 *tomines*. Thus, the annual loss to the royal treasury by virtue of the enlistment of 1,807 tributary *pardos* was 3,765 pesos.[33]

To remedy the situation, the treasury officials recommended nothing less than the elimination of the *pardos* from the militia establishment. In the first place, they contended, no authority existed for their inclusion. To support this argument they cited an order of Viceroy Cruillas issued in 1766 which directed that the companies be composed of whites and "pardos libres". The term "libre" they interpreted to mean free from the obligation to pay tribute since the order conveyed no authority for the enlistment of tributaries. Moreover, there had been no subsequent enactments, royal or viceregal, permitting the employment of tributaries in the companies.

Second, the treasury officials argued that the companies of tributary *pardos* were useless for military purposes. Unlike the units of whites, they were untrained, undisciplined, and without arms or equipment. Even if these deficiencies could be remedied the colored units were unnecessary in peacetime. The seventeen companies of whites were adequate for the maintenance of internal security and, if necessary, they could be augmented by raising other companies of the same class in the provinces listed in the report or in districts where no militia had yet been organized. In the event of war the tributaries could be used to reinforce the whites, but their service could be limited to the duration of the emergency and the loss to the treasury would only be temporary.[34]

On the basis of accumulated testimony and following the recommendations of the *fiscal,* the audiencia prepared a representation to the viceroy showing how the royal treasury and the administration of justice had suffered because of the expansion of the militia in New Galicia.[35] Bucareli, however, apparently took no action on the matter nor, as already remarked, did he make any general decision about the status of the tributary *pardos* in the militia establishment. Instead, it remained for Viceroy Mayorga to come to grips with the problem. After a careful consideration of the points of law involved and of the conflicting demands of fiscal and military policy, Mayorga declared in 1781 that, in time of peace, only those *pardos* enlisted in provincial regiments and battalions and the colored companies of the "coast of Veracruz" who had enjoyed the privilege in the past were granted exemption from tribute. The rest of the militia of New Spain were to be regarded as urban and were exempt only when on active status. To clarify the issue further, those units classified as

provincial were itemized. They were the infantry regiments of
Mexico, Córdova and Jalapa, Tlaxcala and Puebla, and Toluca;
the infantry battalion of Oaxaca; the battalions of *pardos* of Mexico
and Puebla; and the mounted regiments of Puebla and Querétaro.[36]
This declaration was confirmed by royal order with the difference that
tributaries who were enlisted in the legions of San Carlos and Príncipe
were also granted exemption.[37]

Mayorga's enactment, however, did not settle the issue. In complet-
ing the general reorganization of the militia begun by Bucareli,
Mayorga had reformed many of the separate companies of the
Pacific provinces into regiments and battalions. These units now
claimed that their more formal organization entitled them to provincial status. Such was the contention of the Battalion of Infantry
of Valladolid and the Regiment of Dragoons of Michoacán.[38] The
militia of New Galicia, a large part of which had been reorganized
as the Regiment of Infantry of Guadalajara, seized the opportunity
to renew its fight for military privileges and petitioned that the royal
order of October 29, 1781, which denied the *fuero militar* to the
companies of the province, be revoked. Since the unit was now
organized on the model of the older provincial regiments, the
colonel argued that it should enjoy the *fuero* and *preeminencias* of
provincials. Moreover, he alleged, the lack of privileges was seriously
undermining the morale of his men and destroying the regiment.[39]
Inspector General Pascual de Cisneros asserted that the *pardos* of
the Battalion of San Blas had enlisted under the assumption that
they were to enjoy exemption from tribute, but were deserting in
large numbers after discovering that they had been misled.[40]

Other units claimed exception from Mayorga's declaration on
various grounds. The companies of Real de Bolaños stated that their
continuous service in the defense of the frontier of Colotlán gave them
the status of militia on active service;[41] the separate companies of
pardos of Jalapa asserted that as a reward for their services in guarding treasure en route from Mexico to Veracruz they had been granted
exemption from tribute in 1697;[42] and the *alcalde mayor* of Igualapa
reported that despite Mayorga's declaration, he was not collecting
tribute from the *pardo* militiamen of his district because of an exemption conceded to them twenty years earlier.[43]

Mayorga, who tended to take a rather narrow view of the privileges of the militia, in general resisted efforts to extend military exemption from tribute.[44] His position was upheld by the crown.[45] Yet the parties affected tended to press their claims with a persistence that in many cases eventually was rewarded. Mayorga himself conceded exemption to the *pardos* of the militia of Igualapa and San Blas.[46] In 1786 Viceroy Bernardo de Gálvez granted the complete *fuero militar* to both officers and enlisted men of the militia of Tabasco in recognition of their signal services in guarding the coasts of that province.[47] This concession apparently also removed from tributary status the *pardos* enlisted in the several companies. A year later a royal order declared that the *pardos* of the "coasts of Veracruz" were to enjoy the *fuero* of provincials and exemption from tribute. This pronouncement did not, as was the case with Mayorga's earlier declaration, limit exemption to those companies which had enjoyed it in the past.[48] By the beginning of the administration of Revillagigedo the younger, the Battalion of San Blas, the Regiment of Guadalajara, the Battalion of Valladolid, and the Dragoons of Michoacán were regarded as provincials.[49] Presumably this status carried with it the *fuero* of provincials and exemption from tribute for *pardos* enlisted in the several units.

Notes

(PAGE 43)

1. Aguirre Beltrán, pp. 187–190.
2. *Recopilación de Indias,* Lib. III, tít. x, ley 12.
3. Solórzano, Lib. II, cap. xxx, núm. 38.
4. "Instrucción del sr. conde de Revillagigedo al sr. marqués de las Amarillas," *Instrucciones que los vireyes de Nueva España dejaron a sus sucesores,* par. 134, p. 28; Felipe de Zúñiga y Ontiveros, *Calendario manual y guía de forasteros de México, para el año de 1789* . . . , pp. 129–133; "La organización del ejército en Nueva España," 662–663; *Auto acordado* of the audiencia, Guadalajara, September 7, 1772, "Testim.° de los autos principales formados sobre averiguar el perjuicio, q.ᵉ se causa á la R.¹ Haz.ᵃ en el Ramo de Tributos por el establecim.ᵗᵒ de Milicias . . . ," AGN:IG 252 (1772).
5. Royal order, January 5, 1768, AGN:RC 92, no. 9; Bucareli to Arriaga, México, December 27, 1774, AGN:CV 45 (Bucareli), no. 1645.
6. Instructions to Villalba, par. 35.
7. "Nueva formación de Milicias Provinciales, de Valladolid, 1768, AGN:IG 128 (1766–1771); "Estado de la Fuerza . . . de los dos Comp.ˢ . . . una Provincial de Pardos, y otra de Morenos Libres, ultimamente formados . . . ," Veracruz, October 14, 1767, AGN:CV 11 (Croix), no. 294; "Notas que

corresponden al Estado General . . . ," August 23, 1766, AGN:IG 236 (1766); "Dictamen del Brigadier Cavallero de Croix . . . sobre el fixo establecimiento, arreglo, y subsistencia de los Regimientos Provinciales de Infantería y Cavallería," México, September 23, 1771, AGN:CV 1 (Bucareli), no. 25, pars. 29–31.   8. *Bando,* AGN:B 6, no. 87.

9. *Representación* of the *abogado fiscal,* Guadalajara, September 13, 1770, "Testim.° del Quad.ⁿᵒ de autos formados . . . ," AGN:IG 252 (1772). For an account of the legal disabilities of the colored castes, see William H. Dusenberry, "Discriminatory Aspects of Legislation in Colonial Mexico, *The Journal of Negro History,* XXXIII (July, 1948), 284–302.

10. Crespo, "Dictamen," par. 263; Bucareli to Arriaga, México, December 27, 1774, AGN:CV 45 (Bucareli), no. 1645; Revillagigedo to Secretary of State and the General War Office, the Conde del Campo de Alange, México, June 30, 1792, AGN:CV 14 (Revillagigedo), no. 602.

11. I have been unable to find any exact calculation or even an estimate of the annual or accumulated loss to the treasury because of the enlistment of tributaries in the militia. Moreover, in order to arrive at such figures for any given year or period, it would be necessary to compare the individual rosters of all militia companies of the viceroyalty which might contain exempted tributaries with the tribute rolls for the districts in which the companies were raised. This would be a formidable undertaking even if all the documentation were available. The figure given above is based on the very liberal assumption that between 1766 and 1784 the number of tributaries enlisted in the militia might have reached 5,000, that all of these enjoyed exemption, and that all were full tributaries paying two and one-half pesos annually.

12. Fonseca and Urrutía, I, 450.

13. "Plan que demuestra los productos de Real Hacienda en todas las caxas y administraciones de esta Nueva España . . . ," México, July 24, 1771, in José de Gálvez, marqués de Sonora, *Informe general que . . . instruyó y entregó el exmo. sr. marqués de Sonora . . . al exmo. sr. virrey, frey d. Antonio Bucarely y Ursúa . . . ,* Doc. no. 3, preceding p. 191; Alexander von Humboldt, *Ensayo político sobre el reino de la Nueva España,* IV, 146–147.

14. *Recopilación de Indias,* Lib. III, tít. xiv, ley xvii.

15. Lillian Estelle Fisher, *Viceregal Administration in the Spanish-American Colonies,* pp. 95–98.

16. "Instrucción reservada," March 14, 1765, Priestley, p. 404.

17. *Ibid.,* p. 327.

18. *Dictamen* of the *fiscal* of the Audiencia of Mexico, September, 1780, "Copias sobre el Costo de las milicias del Reyno, y su mal estado," AGN:IG 65A (1718–1780).

19. Bucareli to Arriaga, México, December 27, 1774, AGN:CV 45 (Bucareli), no. 1645; Mayorga to José de Gálvez, México, November 28, 1782, AGN:CV 10 (Mayorga), no. 1864; Revillagigedo, *Instrucción reservada,* pars. 589–590; Viceroy the Marqués de Branciforte to Alange, México, September 30, 1794, AGN:CV 2 (Branciforte), no. 66.

20. Fonseca and Urrutía, I, par. 41, pp. 427–428.

21. Gálvez, *Informe,* p. 96; Mayorga to José de Gálvez, México, November 26, 1781, AGN:CV 8 (Mayorga), no. 1380.

22. Gálvez, *Informe,* pp. 96–97.

23. Bucareli to Arriaga, México, December 27, 1774, AGN:CV 45 (Bucareli), no. 1645.

24. *Representación* of the *abogado fiscal,* Guadalajara, September 13, 1770, "Testim.° del Quad.ⁿᵒ de autos formados. . . ." In 1772 there were 17

companies of *españoles* totalling 1,052 men and 24 companies of *pardos* totalling 1,807 (see the table in note 33 of this chapter).

25. *Certificación* of Agapito Martínez, Santa María del Oro, November 18, 1771, "Testim.° de los autos principales. . . . "; roster of the company of *pardos* of Ixtlán, March 31, 1771, *ibid.*

26. Martínez to the treasury officials of New Galicia, [1771], *ibid; auto* of the audiencia, Guadalajara, June 11, 1772, *ibid.*

27. *Consulta,* Tequila, March 2, 1772, *ibid.*

28. *Auto,* Guadalajara, June 11, 1772, *ibid.*

29. *Auto,* Guadalajara, March 10, 1772, *ibid.*

30. Garabito to the Captain General of New Galicia, Guadalajara, March 14, 1772, *ibid.* Garabito was citing the *Ordenanzas de S.M.,* Trat. I, tít. i, arts. 3–4. Article 4 provided that the strength of a fusileer company in an infantry regiment should be three officers and seventy-seven enlisted men.

31. Reply of the *fiscal,* Guadalajara, May 6, 1772, "Testim.° de los autos principales. . . ."

32. *Auto,* Guadalajara, June 11, 1772, *ibid.*

33. *Informe* of the treasury officials, Guadalajara, August 14, 1772. The distribution of companies was as follows:

District	Companies of españoles	Strength	Companies of pardos	Strength	Totals
Tepic and Compostela	2	171	4	300	471
Purificación	1	54	2	108	162
Hostotipaquillo	1	50	1	50	100
Mascota and Guadalajara	4	222	5	415	637
Tequila	1	49	1	55	104
Tequepespan	1	75	1	80	155
Ahuacatlán and Jala	2	102	4	300	402
Acaponeta	2	152	2	169	321
Nieves	1	56	2	166	222
San Sebastián	1	51	1	82	133
Cuquio [?]	1	70	1	82	152
	17	1,052	24	1,807	2,859

34. *Ibid.*

35. *Auto acordado,* Guadalajara, September, 7, 1772, *ibid.*

36. Mayorga to José de Gálvez, México, May 2, 1781, AGN:CV 7 (Mayorga), no. 1050. The particular companies affected and the geographical limits of the "coast of Veracruz" were not specified. The latter term, however, was sometimes used in referring to the Gulf coast from Tampico to the Coatzacoalcos River (see note 48 of this chapter).

37. *Id.* to *id.,* México, March 15, 1782, AGN:CV 9 (Mayorga), no. 1454. A subsequent royal order specifically confirmed the provincial status of the two legions (May 8, 1782, AGN:RC 122, no. 152).

38. Mayorga to José de Gálvez, México, October 10, 1781, AGN:CV 8 (Mayorga), no. 1285.

39. *Id.* to *id.,* México, July 27, 1782, AGN:CV 10 (Mayorga), no. 1721.

40. *Id.* to *id.,* México, November 28, 1782, *ibid.,* no. 1864.

41. *Id.* to *id.,* México, July 27, 1782, *ibid.,* no. 1721.

42. *Id.* to *id.,* México, November 26, 1781, AGN:CV 8 (Mayorga), no. 1380; royal order, May 8, 1782, AGN:RC 122, no. 149.

43. Mayorga to José de Gálvez, México, September 5, 1782, AGN:CV 10 (Mayorga), no. 1779.

44. *Id.* to *id.*, México, October 10, 1781, AGN:CV 8 (Mayorga), no. 1285; *id.* to *id.*, México, November 27, 1781, *ibid.*, no. 1392; *id.* to *id.*, México, January 11, 1782, AGN:CV 9 (Mayorga), no. 1454.

45. The policy of the crown was expressed in a series of royal orders issued on May 8, 1782, AGN:RC 122, nos. 149–153.

46. Mayorga to José de Gálvez, México, September 5, 1782, AGN:CV 10 (Mayorga), no. 1779; *id.* to *id.*, México, November 28, 1782, *ibid.*, no. 1864.

47. *Reglamento provisional para el régimen, gobierno y nueva planta de las milicias de la provincia de Tabasco* (México, 1793), Cap. VIII, art. 5.

48. Royal order, September 1, 1787, AGN:RC 138, no. 2. The scope of this order is not quite clear. It merely stated that the *pardos* of the "coasts of Veracruz" were to enjoy the *fuero* and exemption from tribute in peace as well as war. Insofar as it concerned exemption from tribute, however, Revillagigedo interpreted it to include all the *pardos* enlisted in the militia companies between Tampico and the Coatzacoalcos River and also all those living in communities immediately adjacent to the coast within the same limits who were subject to mobilization in case of emergency but who were not enlisted in the militia (*Reglamento para el régimen, gobierno y nueva planta de las compañías de milicias mixtas del seno que comprehende la provincia de Tampico y Pánuco, hasta el Río Guazacualco. . . .* [México, 1793], Cap. VIII, art. 5).

49. I have seen no specific enactments conceding the status of provincials to the Battalion of San Blas, the Regiment of Guadalajara, the Battalion of Valladolid, and the Dragoons of Michoacán. However, the last two units were listed as provincials by Crespo in 1784 (see Table 3), while all four were regarded as such by Revillagigedo when he assumed office (*Instrucción reservada,* pars. 653–654.)

FIVE

The New Military Program

BY 1780 the army had become an integral part of the institutional structure of New Spain and, as such, the subject of extensive commentary. In regard to its purely military role, observers agreed that the regular component, although somewhat deficient in discipline and morale, was essential to the defense of the realm. Indeed, many senior officers, including viceroys Croix, Bucareli, and Mayorga, advocated a substantial increase in the standing army.[1]* The provincial militia, on the other hand, was severely criticized, and there seems to be little doubt that during the first fifteen years of its existence it was far from an effective military force. Its initial formation by General Villalba was imperfect; it was partially reorganized by Croix, and almost completely reformed by Bucareli and Mayorga. Yet in 1781 and 1782, when war with England made it necessary to mobilize some of the regiments, Mayorga found that most of them were so understrength, poorly trained, and inadequately equipped that they were unfit for active service.[2] Furthermore, in relation to value received the cost of the provincials was high. For in 1780 Mayorga reported that since their formation 2,789,844 pesos had been expended in their upkeep[3]; and in 1784 Inspector General Francisco Crespo calculated that their annual cost amounted to 449,420 pesos.[4] Experience with the urban militia was hardly more encouraging. The Regiment of Commerce of Mexico was so consistently understrength that whenever it was called upon to perform its functions it had to be almost completely reformed.[5] The same deficiencies existed in the other urban units of Mexico and Puebla and in the assorted companies, old and new, existing in those parts of the viceroyalty where no provincials had been raised.[6]

Ineffectiveness and expense were not the only grounds for criticism of the militia. Many civil officials were convinced that its privileges wrought positive damage to the body politic. Instances of such opinions expressed about particular controversies have already been

*Chapter notes begin on page 62.

cited, but testimony of a more general nature is not lacking. In a strongly worded statement, the *fiscal* Areche wrote:

In the provinces where militia exist the *alcaldes mayores* are ignored. They are forced to beg (thus it can be said) for the cooperation of the inhabitants who are enrolled in the companies; they are fearful that they will lose the deference due to their offices; they have suffered the separation of the greatest part of the citizenry from their jurisdictions, and they live in dread that the insubordination [of the militiamen] will be transmitted by example to the Indians. It would not be excessive to believe that their exemption leads to a dangerous lack of respect for the authority of the political chiefs of the provinces.... It can thus be readily seen what the consequences of such a situation will be in small communities where most of the inhabitants are militiamen, in distant provinces where militia is now being organized, and where in general there are inadequate facilities for the prompt enforcement of the law.[7]

The testimony of civil officials was supported by many responsible regular officers. Among the latter was Inspector General Crespo, who was particularly qualified to comment on civil-military relations. Not only was he a professional soldier of rank and reputation, but he had also served six years as *corregidor* of Mexico.[8] In 1784 Crespo prepared the "Dictamen" which has been cited frequently in the preceding pages, and which constituted a detailed and documented critique of the military establishment of New Spain. The privileges of the militia, he charged, were prejudicial to good government. Exemptions from local and royal taxes and charges worked a hardship on less privileged citizens and on municipal officials. Moreover, the militiamen constantly claimed immunities and exemptions which were unauthorized and unjustified. To illustrate his point, Crespo cited the petition of a lieutenant of the urban militia of Guadalajara who, on the grounds of his military privileges, sought to be excused from the contribution of two pesos annually which the Audiencia of New Galicia had levied on all *vecinos* for the support of the poor. The *pardos* enlisted in the militia constituted a special problem. Throughout the viceroyalty they made extravagant allegations of services in order to free themselves from the payment of tribute and to engage in scandalous excesses behind the protection of the *fuero militar*.[9]

Even more serious, continued the inspector, were the innumerable disputes between civil and military officials over the extent and conditions of enjoyment of the *fuero militar*. These resulted in the accumulation of lengthy *competencias* which clogged the viceregal archives, harrassed all levels of government, created needless expenses, and delayed the execution of justice. Moreover, they created dissension and ill-feeling in communities, and undermined the authority and prestige of the *alcaldes mayores*. Finally, Crespo pointed out, as had the *fiscal* of the Audiencia of New Galicia, that the local justices supported themselves with fees and fines, and that when, as the result of widespread enjoyment of the *fuero,* cases were transferred from them to the military jurisdiction, they compensated themselves by increased charges to unprivileged litigants.[10]

Crespo's criticisms were seconded by Manuel Mora, adjutant of the Regiment of Provincial Dragoons of Michoacán. Mora emphasized, however, that disputes and dissensions arose not from the *fuero militar* itself, but because of the intrusion of ignorance and self-interest in its interpretation and administration. In his opinion the blame for such abuses must be shared by militia officers and civil justices. The latter, he charged, refused from the outset to cooperate in the militia program because they received no reward or recognition if they did and no punishment if they did not. Indeed, most of them were actively hostile to the establishment of militia in their jurisdictions since it diminished their authority and made the task of municipal administration more difficult. Their hostility was reflected in their attitude toward the military jurisdiction. "In actions involving militiamen," said Mora, "the ordinary justices refuse to recognize the *fuero militar* or the authority of the militia officers, and commit repeated injustices, excusing themselves, even when shown the royal ordinances, by claiming that these never were officially communicated to them." Furthermore, regulations prescribed that, except in courts-martial cases, military tribunals should follow the procedure used in the ordinary courts in initiating and prosecuting actions against militiamen. But this could not be done because the civil clerks who had to prepare charges and testimony evaded cooperation with the military officials who initiated the action.[11]

On the other hand, Mora charged that the militia officers were

for the most part incompetent, indifferent to their duties, and unfamiliar with the military ordinances. Consequently, they were not
equipped to instruct their men in the character and extent of their
privileges or to act as military judges. When the situation demanded
a defense of the *fuero* they remained idle, but in cases where competence obviously pertained to the ordinary justices, they were
vigorous advocates of the military jurisdiction. In judging cases within
their competence, through ignorance or design they mistook grave
offenses for light ones and administered correspondingly mild punishment or sometimes no punishment at all. As long as militiamen
carried out their military duties, their public and private conduct was
of no concern to their superiors.[12]

Mora illustrated his charge with an example drawn from his own
experience. "Fulano Miliciano," a barber, proposed to open a shop
in his own residence, which was immediately adjacent to the establishment of another barber, a civilian. As the regulations of the
barbers' guild provided that shops should be at least four blocks apart,
the civilian barber appeared before the militiaman's commanding
officer to secure an injunction. The officer regarded the plaintiff's
request as an impertinence, and announced that if the militiaman
wanted to utilize his own home for his business there was no reason
why he should not be allowed to do so. The plaintiff claimed that
he was the victim of discrimination and favoritism. Mora agreed,
asserting that the formation of the militia was certainly undertaken
not to subvert but to support public order and justice. Yet the
officer, when confronted by Mora, stated that the location of barber
shops was inconsequential to the royal service and that he, as a man
of position and honor, should not have to concern himself with such
trifles. Was it any wonder, asked Mora, that militiamen, uninstructed
in the basic principles of military justice, indulged or neglected by their
officers, and seduced by the example of their superiors, should abuse
their privileges?[13]

Other commentators joined in the castigation of militia officers.
Hipólito Villarroel, a former member of the Audiencia of Mexico,
accused them of acquiring their rank and privileges for no other
purpose than to "make sport of justice, avoid payment of their debts,
establish gambling houses, and lead a dissolute life under the pro-

tection of their epaulets."[14] José de Espeleta, who succeeded Crespo as inspector general, complained that some militia officers held commands in nonexistent units, while others lived in the capital or in other parts of the viceroyalty far from their regiments. "They wear the uniform," said Espeleta, "only to enjoy *fueros* and honors and to become eligible for membership in the military orders [of Spain]."[15]

Critics claimed that the privileges of the militia not only affected the ordinary jurisdiction and public order but also the ecclesiastical jurisdiction and private morality. The *fiscal,* Ramón de Posada, charged that the militiamen "even pretend to be exempt from the authority of the curates, to whom all parishioners, without exception, owe obedience in matters spiritual."[16] This charge was elaborated by Adjutant Mora. The license and libertinage of regular officers serving with the militia, he claimed, led the militiamen to believe that fornication was no sin. Under this misapprehension they proceeded to seduce young maidens with false promises of marriage. However, when the injured parties appealed to the church for justice, the curates could obtain no satisfaction from the offenders' superiors, who might simply announce that the militiaman did not want to marry, or rule that the girl did not enjoy a social status equal to that of the soldier, or assert that she came from a poor family which could not provide a suitable dowry. Even if the militiaman wanted to do right by the girl and applied for permission to marry, his request was sometimes refused because in making his application he had not followed the complicated procedures prescribed by regulations. Such circumstances, warned Mora, simply encouraged promiscuity and concubinage.[17]

Inspector General Crespo's analysis of the deficiencies of the military establishment of New Spain induced him to advocate important changes in its organization. Like many other Spanish officers, he believed that the regular garrison was inadequate, and accordingly he proposed that two new regiments of infantry be raised in the viceroyalty. Or, as an alternative, a third regiment might be formed, thus eliminating the need for stationing a peninsular regiment in the colony. The inspector also recommended the formation of a separate battalion of infantry to serve as a permanent garrison for Veracruz.[18] Turning to the provincial militia, Crespo agreed that it was ineffective but believed that deficiencies could be overcome. The principal mistake made in the past, he maintained, was the attempt to raise larger units than the districts assigned for their formation could support. He therefore proposed that the peacetime footing of infantry regiments be reduced from 1,464 to 833 men and that of mounted regiments from 588 to 361 by cutting the strengths of the component companies. Footings could be increased in time of war to 1,361 and 613 for infantry and mounted regiments, respectively, by refilling the companies.[19] In addition to this basic reorganization, the inspector recommended that the legions of San Carlos and Príncipe be reformed as standard infantry and mounted regiments of the provincial class, and that in the viceroyalty at large three elite provincial corps, composed respectively of dragoons, grenadiers, and *cazadores* (light infantry), be raised.[20] The proposed changes would result in an over-all reduction of the peacetime provincial establishment from 16,755 to 11,075 men (compare Tables 3 and 4, Appendix I).

Crespo also proposed a thorough overhauling of the urban militia. The Regiment of Commerce of Mexico, scheduled to be reduced from a regiment of 810 men to a battalion of 407, was to be composed only of merchants serving personally or of employees of contributing merchants, thus eliminating the use of *alquilones*. The Regiment of Commerce of Puebla was to be reorganized on the same footing, while the mounted guild units of the capital were to be formed into a cavalry squadron of three companies, each with a strength of forty-three men. The inspector advocated that the reformed units be granted the *fuero* of provincials, but that its enjoyment be limited to those who served personally.[21]

In addition to the reorganization of the provincials and the urban units of Mexico and Puebla, Crespo proposed the organization of separate companies totalling 2,500 men along the Gulf coast and an equal number in the Pacific provinces. Although these troops would be regarded administratively as urban, functionally they would be classified as coastal. Presumably they were to replace the miscellaneous companies that already existed in the coastal provinces, and were to have as their peacetime mission the maintenance of observation posts and patrols. In wartime they were to delay the advance of an invader until regular or provincial units could arrive in the theater. Because the coastal troops would never be called upon to leave their districts or to serve for extended periods of time, the inspector suggested that they should not enjoy the *fuero militar,* exemption from tribute, or other military privileges except when mobilized.[22]

Finally, Crespo recommended the formation of a fourth class of militia. This was to consist of separate companies of infantry and cavalry which would be raised in the Archbishopric of Mexico and in the bishoprics of Puebla, Valladolid, Oaxaca, and Guadalajara. The districts assigned for their formation were to be those where no provincial or urban units existed or where the population could support additional enlistments. These companies were to have no tactical function but were to serve as a pool of trained manpower which in time of war could be used to bring the regular and provincial regiments to war strength. They would also serve to carry, for purposes of administration and training, the volunteers for the elite provincial corps of grenadiers, dragoons, and *cazadores.* Since the personnel of the replacement companies had few peacetime duties, Crespo felt that they should not enjoy military privileges but suggested that as an exception the provincial *fuero* might be granted to the officers and noncommissioned officers to stimulate their zeal for the service.[23] Presumably, personnel of the elite corps were to enjoy the same privilege since they were classified as provincials. To regularize the organization, administration, and privileges of the reformed militia establishment, the inspector urged that the preparation of a general ordinance be expedited.[24]

In support of his recommendations Crespo argued that the whole militia program would be revitalized by tailoring it to fit the actualities of New Spain. Moreover, the annual cost of maintaining the provincials—by far the most expensive branch of the militia—would be reduced from 449,420 to 275,398 pesos annually.[25] Crespo also emphasized that his plan would reduce, if it did not entirely eliminate, disputes over the privileges of the militia. In the first place, the strength of the provincials would be reduced by approximately a third and the enjoyment of the *fuero* limited to this component and the urban units of Mexico and Puebla. Thus the potential sources of controversy would be substantially diminished. Second, a careful definition of the jurisdictional status of each class of militia in a general ordinance would check unjustified claims and pretensions. By way of summary, the inspector indicated that these measures would re-establish the prestige and authority of civil magistrates, ensure the punishment of offenders, restore the tranquility of communities, equalize municipal burdens, and restore to the treasury the revenue lost through the widespread exemption from tribute of the *pardo* militiamen.[26]

Notes

(PAGES 55–59)

1. Croix to Arriaga, México, January 28, 1769, AGN:CV 13 (Croix), no. 608; "Papel de puntos que ha tenido presentes el Virrey de Nueva España . . . para fundar y asegurar . . . las defensas de estos preciosos Dominios," México, January 29, 1797, AGN:CV 4 (Branciforte, Reservada), no. 752; Mayorga to José de Gálvez, October 5, 1780, AGN:CV 6 (Mayorga), no. 748.

2. A squadron of the Regiment of Cavalry of Querétaro which was ordered to Mexico was unable to make the journey because it lacked satisfactory mounts (Mayorga to José de Gálvez, México, June 2, 1780, AGN:CV 5 [Mayorga], no. 565). When orders were issued for the mobilization of the first battalion of the Regiment of Infantry of Córdova, the viceroy found that it had so many vacancies that it had to be filled with men from the second battalion (*id.* to *id.*, México, January 2, 1782, AGN:CV 9 [Mayorga], no. 1431). When the first battalion of the Regiment of Infantry of Toluca was ordered into active service, the justices failed to cooperate in filling vacancies, and recruiting officers reverted to the practice of dragooning the needed personnel (AGN:IG 7, *passim*). See also Carmen Velázquez, pp. 125–133.

3. Mayorga to José de Gálvez, México, October 5, 1780, AGN:CV 6 (Mayorga), no. 748.

4. "Dictamen," par. 288.

5. Crespo, "Informe," pars. 65–68.

6. Bucareli to Arriaga, México, October 5, 1771, AGN:CV 1 (Bucareli), no. 25; "Dictamen del Marqués de la Torre, Inspector General de Infantería, en punto de Milicias del Reyno de Nueva España . . . ," México, October 24, 1768, AGN:IG 36 (1768–1769), par. 23.

7. Quoted in Crespo, "Dictamen," pars. 267–268. No date is given for the opinion but it was probably written in the late 1770's.

8. *Ibid.*, par. 304.

9. *Ibid.*, pars. 125, 263–265.

10. *Ibid.*, par. 266.

11. "Nueva idea para formar Cuerpos Provinciales en el Reino . . . ," Valladolid, May 25, 1784, AGN:IG 14 (1784–1785). Mora was apparently referring to Tít. VIII, art. 16 of the *Real declaración de milicias provinciales.*

12. "Nueva idea para formar Cuerpos Provinciales en el Reino. . . ."

13. *Ibid.*

14. P. 170.

15. Espeleta to Bernardo de Gálvez, México, October 24, 1785, Biblioteca Nacional de México, MS. 173.

16. Quoted in Crespo, "Dictamen," par. 270.

17. "Nueva idea para formar Cuerpos Provinciales en el Reino. . . ."

18. Crespo, "Dictamen," pars. 147–156. The increase in the over-all strength of the regular component was not so great as might appear since the inspector general proposed that the peacetime footing of infantry regiments be cut from 1,377 to 961 men and of mounted regiments from 522 to 461. This would be accomplished by a reduction in the strength of the component companies. In time of war the regiments could be brought to full strength by refilling the companies.

19. *Ibid.*, pars. 258–261, 273–276, and Quaderno 2.

20. *Ibid.*, pars. 343–345, 358, and Quadernos 2, 5, 8.

21. *Ibid.*, pars. 290–323, and Quaderno 3; Crespo, "Informe," par. 43.

22. Crespo, "Dictamen," pars. 324–331, 357, and Quaderno 4.

23. *Ibid.*, pars. 332–354, 358, and Quaderno 5.

24. *Ibid.*, par. 360.

25. *Ibid.*, pars. 280–289.

26. *Ibid.*, pars. 287–289.

SIX

The Expansion of Military Privilege

THE CROWN approved Crespo's proposals in all their essentials in a series of orders issued between 1786 and 1788. In regard to the regular army, the alternative, suggested by the inspector, of raising three rather than two regiments of infantry was adopted.[1]* The new units—named, respectively, Spain, Mexico, and Puebla— were activated during the administration of Viceroy Manuel Antonio Flores and were ready for service in the summer of 1790.[2] The creation of a third regiment eliminated the need for maintaining substantial numbers of peninsular troops in New Spain. Accordingly, in 1787, the Regiment of Zamora, the Spanish regiment then stationed in the viceroyalty, was ordered to Havana and not replaced.[3] It will be recalled that Crespo also recommended the formation of a separate battalion of regular infantry to serve as a permanent garrison for Veracruz. For reasons not explained the crown suspended approval of this measure, but Viceroy Revillagigedo raised the battalion on his own initiative.[4] Thus the regular component of the Army of New Spain was increased to four regiments and one separate battalion of infantry and two mounted regiments, all of the *fijo* class, plus various auxiliary and presidial units (see Table 5, Appendix I).

A separate order issued in 1788 approved the reorganization of the militia along the lines recommended by Crespo.[5] The arrival of Viceroy Revillagigedo in the fall of 1789, however, not only delayed but changed the character of the reorganization. As a result of his own careful study of the militia question, he found himself disagreeing fundamentally with the most important part of the inspector's plan—that is, the reform of the provincials. He concluded, in short, that not only were they useless in their present state, but that the improvements proposed by Crespo, even if pushed vigorously, would be defeated by the characteristics, distribution, and attitudes of the population.[6] Revillagigedo, moreover, was an outspoken opponent of privileged *fueros* which, he believed, served only to stir up dissen-

*Chapter notes begin on page 71.

sion, obstruct justice, and undermine respect for royal authority.[7] He considered the *fuero* of the provincials to be a particular threat to public order, and, like his predecessors, he deplored the loss of revenue resulting from the enlistment of tributaries.[8] Accordingly, he not only suspended the reorganization of the provincials, but proceeded on his own initiative to disband all existing units except the Regiment of Mexico, the Battalion of Puebla (the second battalion of the Regiment of Tlaxcala and Puebla), the Lancers of Veracruz, and the companies of *pardos* and *morenos* of Veracruz. Mexico and Puebla, he believed, were the only cities in the viceroyalty which had the resources to support provincial regiments, and it was highly desirable to have strong forces in each to keep the unruly population in hand. The colored companies of Veracruz were needed to reinforce the garrison of that port, and the Lancers performed an essential service in patrolling the coast.[9]

Revillagigedo was equally critical of the urban units of Mexico and Puebla. The guild companies of cavalry of Mexico he found to be in reasonably good shape but lacking a definite constitution.[10] These he reorganized, as Crespo recommended, into a cavalry squadron and provided the new formation with a set of regulations governing its organization and administration.[11] The Regiment of Commerce of Mexico, however, was in a deplorable condition. When Inspector General Pedro Gorostiza inspected that unit in 1791, he reported to the viceroy that it was composed mostly of mercenaries, "despreciables por su color y figura," so that out of a reported strength of 608 men hardly a third could be relied upon for effective military service. "In a word," wrote the inspector, "the review could be termed nothing but a ridiculous military farce."[12] Gorostiza also inspected the Regiment of Commerce of Puebla and discovered that, although it had not resorted to the use of *alquilones*, its table of organization called for a strength of 328 men. Only 220 merchants, however, were eligible for enlistment.[13] Revillagigedo was at first inclined to disband both units, but the need to provide security for the two cities in case the regular garrison and the provincial regiments were incorporated in the field army finally induced him to retain them. Both, however, were completely reorganized, the regiment of Mexico as a regiment of 686 men and the Puebla unit as a battalion of 228 men. Each, like the cavalry squadron of Mexico, was provided with its unit regulations.[14]

The renovation of the urban units revived the question of their privileges. Revillagigedo, despite his abhorrence of extraordinary jurisdictions, felt that they were entitled to the *fuero* of provincials, and consequently a rather complicated version of this privilege was conceded to the Battalion of Commerce of Puebla and the Squadron of Guild Cavalry of Mexico. More precisely, when the units were inactive, officers enjoyed the civil and criminal *fueros*; owners of establishments who theoretically comprised the enlisted strength were conceded the criminal whether or not they served personally; substitutes possessed neither the civil nor the criminal. When the units were mobilized, officers continued to enjoy both the civil and the criminal; enlisted men, including both substitutes and owners who served personally, also possessed the complete *fuero*; owners who did not serve in person continued to enjoy only the criminal.[15]

The proposal to grant the provincial *fuero* to the Regiment of Commerce of Mexico reopened old wounds. In a strongly worded protest to the viceroy, the Tribunal of the Consulado reviewed the dispute which had developed between itself and the regiment during the administrations of viceroys Mayorga and Matías de Gálvez. The records, they maintained, proved that the enjoyment of extraordinary jurisdiction by the regiment embarrassed the administration of justice, impeded the transaction of business, and poisoned relations within the community of merchants. Moreover, the question had been settled by the royal order of February 13, 1786, which denied the *fuero militar* to the urban militia of America.[16] Despite the opposition of the consulado, the regulations drawn up for the Regiment of Commerce conceded to it the same privileges enjoyed by the cavalry squadron of the capital and the Battalion of Commerce of Puebla.[17]

Revillagigedo was in fundamental agreement with the rest of Crespo's recommendations for the improvement of the militia. The reform of the coastal units, and particularly those of the Gulf coast, he considered to be a particularly important undertaking because they constituted the first line of defense for the viceroyalty.[18] According-ingly, the 32 companies which reputedly existed between Tampico and the Coatzacoalcos River were reorganized into 22 with a total strength of 2,230 men.[19] This regrouping, it should be added, did not include the Lancers or the companies of *pardos* and *morenos* of Veracruz. These units retained their identities (see Table 5, Appendix I), but were reorganized on a more effective footing.[20] In Tabasco the 27 paper companies of earlier establishment were reformed into 10 with a total strength of 910 men.[21] Along the Pacific coast between Acaponeta and Tehuantepec a similar reorganization was accomplished. Here no fewer than 83 companies of miscellaneous character and irregular constitution existed. These units were regrouped into 41 companies having an over-all strength of 3,550 men.[22]

Revillagigedo also supported Crespo's plan for the organization of separate companies of replacement militia and developed plans for the formation of 115 such units divided into 16 divisions and totalling 9,445 men. During the last months of his administration the division commanders were appointed and recruiting was begun.[23] Finally, Revillagigedo supplemented the proposals of Crespo by organizing a frontier militia. Along the northeastern marches of the viceroyalty, in the provinces of Colotlán, Sierra Gorda, and Nuevo Santander, 19 mounted companies were raised totalling 1,320 men.[24] These were deemed necessary to guard against the depredations of wild Indians and possible intrusions from French Louisiana or the United States.[25]

To provide an incentive and a reward for the personnel of the coastal and frontier militia, Revillagigedo disregarded the recommendations of Crespo and compromised with his own dislike of privileged jurisdictions. The several units and divisions were provisionally conceded the *fuero* and *preeminencias* of provincials and, in addition, the *pardos* enlisted in them were granted exemption from tribute for the duration of their service.[26] Moreover, in conformity with the previously cited royal order of September 1, 1787, the same exemption was conceded to the *pardos* of military age living immediately adjacent to the Gulf of Mexico between Tampico and the Coatzacoalcos River who were not actually enlisted in the companies. In return, however, they were made subject to immediate mobilization in the event of an emergency.[27] The plan of Crespo was followed in regard to the privileges of the separate replacement companies. Only the officers, noncommissioned officers, and attached personnel of the elite corps of dragoons, grenadiers, and light infantry were to enjoy the *fuero* of provincials.[28]

Despite the concession of the *fuero militar* to the urban units of Mexico and Puebla and to the frontier and coastal formations, Revillagigedo's militia program resulted in a substantial contraction of the military jurisdiction. As closely as can be calculated, the number of enlisted militiamen who possessed the criminal *fuero* was reduced from 17,764 to 10,467, and the number of officers enjoying the complete *fuero* from 721 to 439.[29] This result was accomplished by the disbandment of most of the provincials. As for the tribute question, Revillagigedo contended that despite the exemption granted to the frontier and coastal units, there would be an over-all gain in collections because many tributaries lost their exemption through the deactivation of the provincials and the elimination of many of the old coastal companies.[30]

Revillagigedo's efforts to limit the enjoyment of military privilege through the elimination of the provincial militia were frustrated by the policy of his successor, the Marqués de Branciforte. The latter regarded the disbandment as a mistake. Like Crespo, he believed that the provincials could be welded into an effective military force if their personnel was properly selected, trained, and imbued with enthusiasm for the service. Moreover, when he assumed office Spain was at war, and with three of the regular regiments absent from the viceroyalty, he felt that a strong militia establishment was particularly essential.[31] He also maintained that the deactivation of the provincial component was contrary to royal policy since the crown had never rescinded the orders authorizing its reorganization, nor had it approved Revillagigedo's action.[32] Branciforte, therefore, not only recommended to the crown that the provincials be re-established along the general lines advocated by Crespo, but proceeded with the undertaking without awaiting royal approval.[33] It might be added that Branciforte has been accused of being motivated by avarice rather than a sense of duty. Specifically, it was charged that he sold commissions in the reactivated provincial units to individuals who were eager to obtain the *fuero militar* but, instead of using the proceeds to purchase armament, he appropriated them for his own use.[34] It is true that he hoped to finance the militia program from contributions of persons who aspired to be officers.[35] I have found, however, no documentary evidence of misuse of funds.

As the re-establishment progressed, certain changes were made in the number and distribution of units proposed by Crespo. The battalions of *pardos* of Mexico and Puebla were not reactivated because Branciforte, like his predecessor, felt that their privileges were prejudicial to the interests of the treasury, public order, and the administration of justice.[36] Apparently, the formation of the Battalion of Infantry of San Carlos in San Luis Potosí was also abandoned.[37] On the other hand, these reductions were more than compensated for by the establishment of provincial units not included in Crespo's plan. In the province of Celaya, Branciforte raised a full regiment of infantry.[38] San Miguel el Grande, however, which was in the area marked out for recruiting, was not willing to play a secondary role. It petitioned the viceroy that, in addition to furnishing its quota of infantrymen, it be allowed to raise its own regiment of dragoons, to be called the Regiment of the Queen. The city of Puebla, instead of providing a battalion for the Regiment of Infantry of Tlaxcala and Puebla, offered to raise a regiment of its own, while the Governor of Tlaxcala, not to be outdone, proposed that a full regiment be formed in his province. The viceroy enthusiastically accepted these offers.[39] In addition, Branciforte decided to raise a regiment of dragoons and a battalion of infantry in New Galicia and to increase to a regiment the battalion of infantry scheduled to be formed in Valladolid.[40] Thus by the end of his administration there were formed, or forming, seven regiments and three separate battalions of provincial infantry, eight mounted regiments, the Lancers of Veracruz, and the companies of *pardos* and *morenos* of Veracruz. Compared with Crespo's proposed four regiments and six separate battalions of infantry, six mounted regiments, and the provincial units of Veracruz, Branciforte's program meant a net increase in the provincial establishment of three battalions of infantry and two mounted regiments (compare Tables 4 and 5, Appendix I).

The reorganization described in the preceding pages established the Army of New Spain on a footing which remained virtually unchanged until the movement for independence. It also led to a substantial expansion of the military jurisdiction. Inspector General

Crespo, its original promoter, had envisioned as one of its objectives a reduction in the number of persons enjoying the *fuero militar*. The reorganization of the urban, coastal, and frontier militia by Revilla-gigedo, and the re-establishment and increase of the provincials during the administration of Branciforte produced the opposite results. By 1800 some 20,329 enlisted militiamen enjoyed the criminal *fuero* and some 1,054 officers the complete *fuero*.[41] As emphasized earlier in this study, more important than mere numbers was the fact that the military jurisdiction was established in nearly every province and, indeed, in nearly every community in the viceroyalty.

A further extension of the military jurisdiction resulted from the fact that between 1794 and 1808, almost constant fears of invasion led to frequent mobilizations of units of the militia. The Regiment of Commerce of Mexico was on active duty without intermission from May 10, 1794, to February 21, 1802. The Squadron of Guild Cavalry of Mexico was mobilized from November 12, 1795, to January 17, 1796, and again from February 18, 1797, to February 24, 1802.[42] The provincials were also used extensively. In May, 1793, Revillagigedo ordered the Provincial Regiment of Mexico to active duty,[43] and in December, 1796, the danger of war with England led to the mobiliza-tion of the entire provincial establishment for training and for in-corporation into the field army if necessary.[44]

When, in January, 1797, word arrived in New Spain that war had been declared, the provincial infantry regiments of Mexico, Toluca, Tlaxcala, Córdova, and Celaya were ordered to join the army of operations bivouacked in Córdova, Orizaba, Jalapa, and Perote.[45] In the summer of the same year, these units were joined by the Battalion of Provincial Infantry of Oaxaca and the Dragoons of Puebla. Other provincial units and the metropolitan urban corps were used to gar-rison Mexico, Puebla, and Veracruz.[46] At the same time, the Dragoons of San Luis and San Carlos and the mounted companies of Nuevo León and Nuevo Santander were incorporated into the "Army of the North," which was centered at San Luis Potosí and which had as its mission the defense of the northeastern frontier in case the United States, as was feared, should ally itself with Great Britain and attack New Spain.[47] Most of the provincial units were returned to inactive status by Viceroy Azanza in the summer of 1798,[48] but the renewal of war with England in 1805 led to another general mobilization which lasted from May of that year until November, 1808.[49] These frequent and protracted mobilizations of the militia meant that for their duration not only officers and their dependents, but also enlisted men and their dependents enjoyed the complete *fuero militar.*[50]

Notes

(PAGES 64–66)

1. Royal orders, September 25, 1786, AGN:RC 135, no. 60; September 24, 1787, AGN:RC 138, no. 46; May 5, 1788, AGN:RC 140, no. 14.
2. Flores to Antonio Valdés, México, May 24, 1788, AGN:CV 2 (Flores), no. 352; Revillagigedo, *Instrucción reservada,* par. 543.
3. Royal order, September 25, 1787, AGN:RC 138, no. 152.
4. *Instrucción reservada,* par. 561.
5. October 20, 1788, AGN:RC 141, no. 106.
6. Revillagigedo to Alange, México, February 6, 1790, AGN:CV 22 (Revillagigedo, Reservada), no. 296, pars. 1–29; *Instrucción reservada,* pars. 574, 588.
7. *Instrucción reservada,* pars. 92, 117–119.
8. *Ibid.,* par. 574; Revillagigedo to Alange, México, February 6, 1790, AGN:CV 22 (Revillagigedo, Reservada), no. 296, pars. 43, 56; *id.* to *id.,* México, June 30, 1792, AGN:CV 14 (Revillagigedo), no. 602; *id.* to *id.,* México, January 3, 1792, AGN:CV 25 (Revillagigedo, Reservada), no. 469.
9. Revillagigedo to Alange, México, February 6, 1790, AGN:CV 22 (Revillagigedo, Reservada), no. 296, pars. 31, 39–42; *Instrucción reservada,* pars. 581–582, 602–604.
10. *Instrucción reservada,* pars. 585–586; Revillagigedo to Alange, México, September 26, 1790, AGN:CV 6 (Revillagigedo), no. 55.
11. *Reglamento provisional para el régimen, gobierno y subsistencia del esquadrón urbano de caballería que de las antiguas compañias de los tratantes de panadería, tocinería y curtiduría, se ha formado en esta capital* (México, 1790).
12. México, October 8, 1791, "Sobre dar nueba forma al Regimiento Urbano del Comercio de Mexico," AGN:IG 122 (1783–1894 [*sic*]).
13. Revillagigedo, *Instrucción reservada,* par. 614; Revillagigedo to Alange, México, September 30, 1793, AGN:CV 18 (Revillagigedo), no. 1017.
14. Revillagigedo to Alange, México, February 6, 1790, AGN:CV 22 (Revillagigedo, Reservada), no. 296, pars. 59–66; *Instrucción reservada,* 610–615; *Reglamento provisional para el régimen, gobierno y subsistencia del regimiento de infantería urbano del comercio de esta capital* (México, 1793); *Reglamento provisional para el régimen, gobierno, y nueva planta del cuerpo de infantería urbano del comercio de Puebla* (México, [1793?]).
15. *Reglamento provisional . . . del esquadrón urbano de caballería . . . ,* arts. 34–37; *Reglamento provisional . . . del cuerpo de infantería urbano del comercio de Puebla,* arts. 28–30.
16. México, November 28, 1791, "Sobre dar nueba forma al Regimiento Urbano del Comercio de Mexico."

17. *Reglamento provisional* . . . *del regimiento de infantería urbano del comercio de esta capital*, arts. 37–39.

18. *Instrucción reservada*, pars. 606, 616.   19. *Ibid.*, par. 605.

20. *Ibid.*, par. 581.   21. *Ibid.*, par. 599.   22. *Ibid.*, pars. 616–625.

23. *Ibid.*, pars. 628–646; Revillagigedo to Alange, México, June 28, 1794, AGN:CV 22 (Revillagigedo), no. 1225.

24. *Instrucción reservada*, pars. 592–598.

25. Revillagigedo to Alange, México, May 29, 1793, AGN:CV 18 (Revillagigedo), no. 875.

26. *Instrucción reservada*, pars. 594, 598, 601, 607; Revillagigedo to Alange, México, December 31, 1793, AGN:CV 18 (Revillagigedo), no. 1086; *Reglamento para el régimen, gobierno y nueva planta de las compañías de milicias mixtas del seno que comprehende la provincia de Tampico y Pánuco, hasta el Río Guazacualco.* . . . '(México, 1793), Cap. VIII, arts. 1–4, 10–11; *Reglamento provisional para el régimen, gobierno y nueva planta de las compañías de milicias de la costa del sur del reyno de Nueva España.* . . . (México, 1793), Cap. VIII, arts. 1–7; *Reglamento provisional para el cuerpo de milicias de caballería, que con el nombre de la Frontera de la colonia del Nuevo Santander, debe formarse en la jurisdicción de los valles y partido de Ríoverde.* . . . (México, 1793), Cap. VI, arts. 1–11; *Reglamento provisional para el régimen y gobierno del cuerpo de milicias de caballería que con el nombre de Frontera de Sierra-Gorda ha de arreglarse en las jurisdicciones de Cadereyta, San Luis de la Paz, Presidio de Xalaca pertenecinte á la de Mextitlán.* . . . (México, 1793), Cap. VI, arts. 1–7. In the case of the companies of Tabasco, both officers and enlisted men were granted the complete *fuero militar* in conformity with the previously cited decree issued by Viceroy Bernardo de Gálvez on April 29, 1786 (*Reglamento provisional para el régimen, gobierno y nueva planta de las milicias de la provincia de Tabasco* [México, 1793], Cap. VIII, art. 5).

27. *Reglamento para* . . . *las compañías* . . . *de Tampico y Pánuco, hasta el Río Guazacualco* . . . , Cap. VIII, arts. 5–6.

28. *Instrucción que debe observar el subdelegado de* ——— *para la creación de compañías sueltas de milicias en el distrito de su jurisdicción* (México, January 7, 1797), "Documentacion sobre compañias sueltas de milicias," AGN:IG 312 (1791–1797), art. 35.

29. The first set of figures is based on Revillagigedo's report on the strength of the militia when he assumed office. (*Instrucción reservada*, pars. 653–657). They include only those units classified by the viceroy as provincial since, as related in Chapters II and III, most of the urban militia was denied the *fuero militar*. The postreorganization figures are derived from the strength of the militia at the end of Revillagigedo's administration (*ibid.*, pars. 581, 585, 593–597, 599, 602–603, 605, 611, 615, 624, 647 and from *reglamentos* cited in notes 26 and 27 above). In this case, all militia units except the replacement companies are counted because, by virtue of their several *reglamentos*, they all enjoyed the *fuero* of provincials. Although, as noted above, certain individuals in the replacement companies were to enjoy the *fuero militar*, this component had just begun to be organized when Revillagigedo left office so that the numbers involved would be impossible to determine and in any case would not appreciably affect the totals. Both sets of figures, it must be added, are only approximate because they do not take into account a number of unknowns whose values are almost impossible to calculate. Both presume that units counted were at full strength. Such was probably not the case, particularly with the prereorganization totals. Neither

include an indeterminate number of dependents who possessed the *fuero* in varying degrees. Moreover, the prereorganization figures do not include coastal and frontier units which enjoyed or claimed to enjoy the privilege by special dispensation. I believe, however, that the basic proportion of the two sets of figures is approximately correct and that Revillagigedo accomplished a substantial reduction in the number of individuals who enjoyed the *fuero* of provincials.

30. Revillagigedo to Alange, México, June 29, 1793, AGN:CV 18 (Revillagigedo), no. 925. The soundness of Revillagigedo's contention is difficult to prove or disprove. As stated earlier (Chapter IV, note 11), I have been unable to find any record or to make any calculation of the number of tributaries enlisted in the militia or of the over-all losses to the royal treasury as a result of such enlistment for any given year or period before the reorganization undertaken by Revillagigedo. Moreover, such figures would tend to fluctuate because of desertions, discharges, new enlistments, and the vacillating and selective policy of the crown in granting and withdrawing the privilege of exemption (see Chapter IV, *passim*). A postreorganization figure is also difficult to arrive at. Presumably, no tributaries were admitted into the remaining provincial regiments. However, the *reglamento* of the militia of the Pacific Coast shows that of the 3,550 men to be enlisted, 3,190, or about 90 per cent, were to be *pardos* (Annex 1 to the *reglamento*). If the same percentage were taken of the 3,140 men to be enlisted on the Gulf coast including Tabasco, and I believe that such a percentage would be approximately correct, some 2,826 would be *pardos*. If to the totals of the coastal divisions be added the 210 men of the companies of *pardos* and *morenos* of Veracruz and the 324 men of the Lancers of Veracruz, which were probably all *pardos*, a grand total of some 6,550 *pardos* enlisted in the coastal militia results. If all these were full tributaries subject to the levy of two and one-half pesos, the annual loss to the royal treasury would be 16,375 pesos. This figure presumes that the coastal units were maintained at full strength, which was probably not the case. But it does not include an indeterminate number of tributaries living on the Gulf coast who were not actually enrolled in companies, but who were subject to mobilization in case of war and were thus exempt. Moreover, it is not a total for the entire viceroyalty because it does not include an indeterminate number of tributaries who were apparently enlisted in the frontier corps of Colotlán and Nuevo Santander (Revillagigedo, *Instrucción reservada*, pars. 594, 598). In view of these uncertainties, any pronouncement as to whether Revillagigedo's reorganization of the militia resulted in a net gain or loss to the *ramo de tributos* would be an unsupported guess.

31. "Instrucción del virey marqués de Branciforte a su sucesor don Miguel José de Azanza," Orizaba, March 16, 1797, *Instrucciones que los vireyes de Nueva España dejaron a sus sucesores*, pars. 34–41, pp. 133–134; Branciforte to Alange, México, October 5, 1794, AGN:CV 1 (Branciforte, Reservada), no. 81. In the summer of 1793, the regiments of infantry of New Spain and Mexico had been ordered to Havana and there placed under the command of the Captain General of Cuba for operations against the French in the Caribbean (Revillagigedo, *Instrucción reservada*, par. 561; Revillagigedo to Alange, México, October 5, 1793, AGN:CV 18 [Revillagigedo], no. 876). The Regiment of Puebla followed in 1794 (Branciforte to Alange, México, October 6, 1794, AGN:CV 2 [Branciforte], no. 66).

32. Branciforte to Alange, México, July 30, 1794, AGN:CV 1 (Branciforte, Reservada), no. 22.

33. *Id.* to *id.*, México, October 5, 1794, *ibid.*, no. 81; "Relacion de los Cuerpos Provinciales extinguidos . . . que van a restablecerse . . . ," México, December 5, 1794, *ibid.*, no. 134.

34. Hubert Howe Bancroft, *History of Mexico,* III, 408, n. 21; Andrés Cavo, *Los tres siglos de Méjico durante el gobierno español* . . . , p. 639.

35. "Instrucción del . . . marqués de Branciforte a . . . Azanza," par. 46; Branciforte to Alange, México, April 6, 1795, AGN:CV 1 (Branciforte, Reservada), no. 242.

36. Branciforte to Alange, México, September 30, 1794, AGN:CV 2 (Branciforte), no. 66.

37. "Estado que demuestra . . . los Cuerpos Provinciales . . . que han vuelto a formarse . . . ," México, October 31, 1795, AGN:CV 2 (Branciforte), no. 416.

38. *Ibid.*

39. Branciforte to Alange, México, January 15 and October 31, 1795, AGN:CV 2 (Branciforte, Reservada), nos. 160, 413.

40. Branciforte to Secretary of State and the General War Office, Juan Manuel Alvarez, Orizaba, July 30, 1797, AGN:CV 4(Branciforte, Reservada), no. 871; "Estado q.^{e} manifiesta el pie y fuerza en q.^{e} se ha establecido el Regim.^{to} Prov.^{l} de Inf.^{a} de Valladolid . . . ," Orizaba, November 20, 1797, AGN:CV 11 (Branciforte), no. 949.

41. The figures cited are the total table of organization strengths of militia officers and militiamen in the provincial, urban, coastal, and frontier divisions as shown in Table 5, with the exception that the 3,000 men of the companies of Nuevo León and Nuevo Santander are not included. I have not found any information on the jurisdictional status of these companies. The selected individuals in the replacement companies who enjoyed the *fuero* of provincials are not included because that branch of the militia was in the process of formation and the number of persons affected would be almost impossible to calculate. Actually, the figures are only approximations because of the constant change in unit strengths resulting from discharges, desertions, and new enlistments, and because of the unknown factors mentioned above.

42. Viceroy Félix Berenguer de Marquina to Secretary of State and the General War Office, Joseph Antonio Caballero, México, February 26, 1802, AGN:CV 9 (Marquina), no. 518; *id.* to *id.*, México, February 26, 1802, *ibid.*, no. 519.

43. Revillagigedo to Alange, México, May 29, 1793, AGN:CV 18 (Revillagigedo), no. 869.

44. Branciforte to Azanza, México, December 28, 1796, AGN:CV 8 (Branciforte), no. 717.

45. Branciforte to Alvarez, Orizaba, May 31, 1797, AGN:CV 4 (Branciforte, Reservada), no. 821; *id.* to *id.*, Orizaba, July 30, 1797, *ibid.*, no. 874; "Papel de puntos que ha tenido presentes el Virrey de Nueva España . . . para fundar y asegurar . . . las defensas de estos preciosos Dominios," México, January 29, 1797, *ibid.*, no. 752, par. 34; Branciforte to Azanza, México, February 26, 1797, *ibid.*, no. 783.

46. Branciforte to Alvarez, Orizaba, December 30, 1797, *ibid.*, no. 973; "Instrucción . . . del marqués de Branciforte a . . . Azanza," pars. 48–50, p. 135.

47. Branciforte to Alvarez, Orizaba, June 30, 1797, AGN:CV 4 (Branciforte, Reservada), no. 845; *id.* to *id.*, Orizaba, July 30, 1797, *ibid.*, no. 874; Bancroft, III, 491.

48. Cavo, p. 645.

49. Viceroy José de Iturrigaray to Caballero, México, May 7, 1805, AGN:CV 13 (Iturrigaray), no. 814; "Estado que manifiesta las Tropas que hay puestas sobre las Armas . . . ," [1808?], AGN:H 521, fols. 194v–195; *Gazeta de México*, XIII (no. 24, Saturday, March 22, 1806), 196; *ibid.*, XIII (no. 92, Wednesday, November 12, 1806), 756; *ibid.*, XV (no. 15, Wednesday, February 17, 1808), 115–117; Pedro Garibay to the intendant of the bivouac, November 6/8, 1808, Archivo Histórico de Hacienda, Leg. 585–84.

50. *Real declaración de milicias provinciales*, Tít. VII, art. 29; "Reglamento Provicional de Milicias de Villa de Córdoba y Xalapa," Cap. VI, art. 21.

SEVEN

The Royal Decree of February 9, 1793

INSPECTOR GENERAL CRESPO, it will be recalled, hoped to minimize civil-military disputes by the preparation of a general ordinance defining and delimiting the privileges of the militia. Although the project was never consummated, Revillagigedo did prepare a series of special regulations which prescribed the *fuero* and *pre-eminencias* of the units he reorganized. Efforts to control disputes by this approach, however, were frustrated by two factors. In the first place, the several regulations were provisional in character and required the approval of the crown before having the full force of law. Thus, any viceregal decisions based on them were also provisional, and the way was left open for appeals, demurrers, and delays pending royal action. Second, even the most specific and precisely worded definition of privileges was not proof against the ingenuity of disputing parties in interpreting regulations to their own advantage.

These propensities are well illustrated by a controversy which began during the administration of Revillagigedo and continued into that of Viceroy Azanza. The source of the dispute was the interpretation of the royal decree of February 9, 1793. Although parts of this enactment have been quoted previously, it is worth reproducing in full, not only because an understanding of its contents is necessary to follow the development of the dispute, but also because it is one of the key documents illustrating the character and history of the *fuero militar*. It reads as follows:

The considerable understrength suffered by the army for many years made it necessary to draft 12,000 men from the militia in 1770 and to institute general levies in 1773, 1775, and 1776, to fill the vacancies. This situation can be attributed, according to the reports of various senior officers and the representations of my *Consejo Supremo de Guerra,* to the contraction, in many cases, of the *fuero* and privileges conceded to military personnel by my august predecessors since the reigns of the kings Charles I and Philip II. Moreover, my attention has been called to the grave injuries to the State and the discipline of my troops because of the disputes which so frequently arise between the military and other jurisdictions. These occupy a large part of the time of my attorneys and ministers of the superior tribunals and, while they are being settled, result in the delay in the punishment of the guilty and the extended imprisonment of the innocent. I have reflected on the matter with the care it deserves and desire to show in as many ways as possible the proper attention to those vassals who, abandoning their homes and private interests and suffering the rigorous fatigues of war, are ready to sacrifice their lives in defense of the State. I desire also that these individuals not be left in a legal status inferior to those who, because they are not enlisted, can be summoned only before their own civil justices.

I have resolved, therefore, that to stop all jurisdictional disputes at their origins, military magistrates will have in the future private and exclusive cognizance of all cases, civil and criminal, which are brought against personnel of my army and of all official summons, excepting only actions dealing with *mayorazgos* and with the division of inheritances provided such inheritances do not derive from testamentary dispositions of soldiers. Furthermore, I order that *competencias* [with the military jurisdiction] may not be formed or admitted by any judge or tribunal on any account or on any pretext, and that all *competencias* pending, both civil and criminal, be regarded as terminated and closed. Judges and tribunals with whom such *competencias* have been formed will forward the records to the military jurisdiction so that its tribunals can proceed according to ordinance in cases of military offenses and according to general laws and dispositions in civil and criminal actions arising from ordinary law. In the interests of prompt action, ordinary magistrates may arrest military personnel, but they must form a summary of the case and forward it immediately, along with the prisoner, to the nearest military judge. All the above provisions will be observed regardless of any existing dispositions, royal resolutions, orders, pragmatics, cedulas, and decrees, all of which, regardless of their character, *de motu propio, cierta ciencia,* and by my own authority and royal power, I revoke, abrogate, and annul. I order, however, that in the future, the penalties established in the cited cedulas, pragmatics, royal decrees, and resolutions remain in force, but that they be imposed on the personnel of my army only by military judges since this is my considered royal will. . . .[1]*

*Chapter notes begin on page 89.

Insofar as the regular army was concerned, the intent of the decree
is quite clear. It was designed to stimulate interest in military service
by amplifying the *fuero militar*. All cases of *desafuero,* with the
exception of the two specifically stated, were abolished.[2] Moreover,
the categorical nature of the enactment, the reiteration of its purpose,
and the emphasis on the deliberate and absolute character of the
authority behind it all suggest that the crown was trying in advance
to prevent evasions and misinterpretations. Questions inevitably arose,
however, about its application to the militia. Did the term, "personnel
of my army" (*Individuos de mi Exército*) include the militia? If so,
was it intended only that the *fuero* which the militia already enjoyed—
the criminal and civil class for officers and the criminal class for enlisted men—be amplified by the elimination of all cases of *desafuero*
except two? Or, in addition, did the provision that in the future military judges should have private and exclusive jurisdiction in civil and
criminal actions against personnel of the army mean that both officers
and men of the militia now enjoyed the complete *fuero* even when
not on active duty?

These questions were posed in a barrage of inquiries, claims, and
disputes which descended on Viceroy Revillagigedo after the publication of the decree in New Spain.[3] For example, the *alcalde de corte,*
Francisco Saavedra, had pending before him a civil action lodged
by certain creditors against Pedro de Valle, a baker and soldier of
the Squadron of Guild Cavalry of Mexico. Pedro Verduga Blanco,
commander of the squadron, maintained that the decree in effect
conceded the civil *fuero* to enlisted men of the militia and that he
had jurisdiction in the case of Valle. He therefore requested Saavedra
to forward, in accordance with the terms of the enactment, the
records of the case to his tribunal and to remand the prisoner to his
custody.[4]

Saavedra refused to comply and appealed to the viceroy. Valle's
case, he declared, was but one of many civil actions against urban
militiamen which came before him for settlement. It was not his
purpose to deny the commandant his proper jurisdiction or to foment
disputes. Nevertheless, there were grave doubts in his mind as to
whether the royal enactment was intended to apply to the urban
militia. In the first place, it specifically distinguished between the army

and the militia when it stated that it had been necessary to draft men from the militia (*hombres de Milicias*) into the army (*el Exército*). Therefore when the term "army" was used again in the statement that only military magistrates can take cognizance of civil and military actions brought against "personnel of my army" (*Individuos de mi Exército*), it was not meant to include the militia but referred only to the regular army. Furthermore, Saavedra maintained, the decree specifically stated that the crown wished to compensate "those vassals who, abandoning their homes and private interests and suffering the rigorous fatigues of war, are ready to sacrifice their lives in defense of the State." Certainly the urban troops which were never called upon to leave their homes even in time of war did not fall in that category. In the opinion of Saavedra, if the decree applied at all to urban militiamen, it merely abolished the cases of *desafuero* within the *fuero* which they already enjoyed.[5]

Verduga also presented his case to the viceroy. It is, however, more interesting as an illustration of how jurisdictional disputes aroused passions than as an example of closely reasoned legal argument. Verduga charged that, despite His Majesty's desire to eliminate jurisdictional disputes, Saavedra, through his misinterpretation of the royal decree, was introducing new dissensions and injustices. The affairs of Valle, for example, were nearly ruined by the *competencia* arising from his arrest. Many other cases had arisen in which personnel of the urban militia had suffered because of the delays and disputes promoted by ordinary justices. Moreover, the latter were motivated not by any legitimate doubts about jurisdiction but only by self-interest.[6]

As might be expected, the Regiment of Commerce of Mexico soon entered the lists. Its involvement arose from several cases, the most interesting of which was a criminal action instigated by Manuel Antonio Santa María y Escovedo, judge of the *Tribunal de la Acordada*, against José Ramírez de Roxas, a soldier of the regiment, for the sale of prohibited beverages. Colonel Antonio de Rabago, the regimental commander, demanded in very strong terms that the case be transferred to his jurisdiction in accordance with the terms of the royal decree. Santa María refused to comply, apparently on the grounds that Ramírez' offense was a case of *desafuero*. To Rabago he replied that, according to his interpretation, the enactment spoke only of members of the army (*Individuos de Exército*) and not of the urban militia. He suggested, therefore, that the accused be tried in his court as provided by existing enactments. If this suggestion met with the colonel's approval, he promised to conclude the case promptly so as to minimize the inconvenience to Ramírez. He requested, however, that if Rabago persisted in the views expressed in his demand, the colonel should proceed with the proper moderation and respect.[7]

At the same time, Santa María wrote to Revillagigedo justifying his stand. Like the *alcalde de corte*, Saavedra, he maintained that the decree distinguished between the army and the militia, and that it was the crown's intention to reward only those who made extensive personal sacrifices in the royal service. To strengthen his case he asserted that since the publication of the enactment in the capital and because of the interpretation placed on it by the colonel, members of the regiment believed themselves exempt from the authority of the *Tribunal de la Acordada*. This was evidenced by the discovery of *chinguirito* in three wineshops belonging to soldiers of the regiment.[8]

Rabago, upon receiving a copy of Santa María's representation, proceeded to present his own case to the viceroy. The king, he argued, realizing that exemption from the ordinary jurisdiction was a privilege highly regarded by soldiers, had issued the decree to amplify their *fuero* and stimulate their loyalty and their enthusiasm for the service. There could be no doubt that he had intended thus to reward and inspire the militia as well as the regular army. In regard to his own command in particular, Rabago asserted that the Regiment of Commerce had always been prompt to respond to the call to arms and had performed its service at its own expense and without cost to the royal treasury. In recognition of its zeal and loyalty, the king had distinguished it above other urban units by granting its officers royal commissions signed by his own hand. Could it be believed, asked the colonel, that it was now His Majesty's wish to disgrace the regiment he had once honored by denying the *fuero* to it alone of all the militia establishment and exposing its soldiers to the contempt and abuse of all the ordinary justices? On the contrary, the regiment now enjoyed the *fuero militar* in all its amplitude by virtue of the decree, and Santa María's arguments were offensive and impertinent. Having thus established through an ingenious divination of the royal intent that the decree applied equally to the regular army and the Regiment of Commerce, Rabago proceeded to more specific points. Santa María's proposal to handle the case of Ramírez according to existing ordinances was, he maintained, based on error, since the decree by its very wording superseded all previous enactments. Moreover, if the king had wanted to deny jurisdiction over traffic in prohibited beverages to the military courts, he would have done so specifically just as he had in cases involving entailed estates and inheritances.[9]

Uncertainties about the interpretation of the decree were not limited to the capital. Shortly after its publication in New Spain, Phelipe Díaz de Hortega, the Intendant of Valladolid, received an inquiry from the *subdelegado* of Zinapécuaro, Roques Sánches de Andrade. Sánches stated that he was preparing to proclaim the enactment in his district. But in view of the fact that it spoke only of personnel of the army, he wished to know whether it affected the status of the militia and, more specifically, whether it conceded the civil *fuero* to enlisted men.[10] A similar request was received by Manuel de Flon, Governor-Intendant of Puebla, from the *subdelegado* of Guayacocotla.[11] Both queries were forwarded to the viceroy.[12] A more specific problem was raised by Bruno Díaz de Salcedo, the Intendant of San Luis Potosí. Díaz stated that in the intendancy a number of cases were pending against officers of the Legion of San Carlos for fraud against the royal treasury. Among them was an action brought by the Administrator of Tobacco, Powder, and Playing Cards, against José Díaz Bustillo, a resident of Ríoverde, for the sale of fireworks made from contraband powder. Ordinances defined defrauding the treasury as a case of *desafuero*. Yet, continued the intendant, the attorney of the defendant demanded that the case be remanded to the commander of the Legion on the grounds that the royal decree conceded to the appropriate military magistrate exclusive jurisdiction in all civil and criminal actions against military personnel, with the two specified exceptions. Intendant Díaz reported that because of the doubts raised by the attorney's request, he had suspended action in the suit until the viceroy clarified the jurisdictional status of the militia.[13]

As was customary in cases of disputes over the privileges of the militia, Revillagigedo submitted the questions raised by the royal decree to the *auditor de guerra* and to the inspector general for opinions. These two officials, however, found themselves in fundamental disagreement. Gorostiza, the inspector, was of the opinion that the decree affected the militia, but only to the extent of eliminating cases of *desafuero* within the *fuero* which it already enjoyed. In no sense did it concede a new *fuero*—the civil—to enlisted militiamen. To assume that in peacetime the militia should have the same privileges as regulars was, in the inspector's opinion, contrary to the spirit of the enactment and the dictates of reason. While militiamen remained at home and attended to their private interests, regulars served continuously and were therefore more deserving of royal favor.[14] The *auditor*, on the other hand, interpreted the decree as conceding the complete *fuero* in all its amplitude both to officers and enlisted men of the militia and, as far as privileges were concerned, placing the militia on a status equal to regulars.[15] Revillagigedo agreed with Gorostiza, and on July 6, 1793, issued an interim opinion to the effect that the royal decree applied only to the regular army, and that the militia enjoyed and would continue to enjoy only that *fuero* granted by previous enactments.[16] At the same time he requested the crown to clarify the decree.[17]

Before the crown acted, the controversy was reopened. In November, 1794, a new *auditor de guerra* submitted to Viceroy Branciforte a memorandum charging that the tribunals of the viceroyalty were not remitting civil and criminal actions against military personnel to the military jurisdiction as commanded by the royal decree. The *auditor* recommended that this provision be enforced.[18] Branciforte accepted the recommendation and ordered that all such actions pending, or which might arise in the future, be sent to the office of the captain general without delay.[19] The order, however, failed to distinguish between actions against regulars and actions against militiamen. Thus it could be interpreted to mean that Branciforte understood the decree as applying equally to both components and that he was, in effect, reversing the position taken by Revillagigedo.

Such was the apprehension of that perennial enemy of the *fuero militar*, the Tribunal of the Consulado. In a communication to

Branciforte, that body maintained that the viceregal order should not and could not apply to mercantile actions against members of the Regiment of Commerce. Citing Roman and feudal precedents, it developed the argument that corporations governed by special laws and usages must possess their private courts, members of which were familiar with those laws and usages. Otherwise, delays and miscarriages of justice would be inevitable. Thus, the Tribunal of the Consulado had been established primarily to provide the community of merchants with magistrates who were familiar with mercantile law and who could settle commercial cases with fairness and dispatch. However, continued the tribunal, in Mexico City nearly all merchants were enrolled in the Regiment of Commerce. If Branciforte's order were to apply to mercantile actions against militiamen, the tribunal would be deprived of its principal function. At the same time, such actions would be heard by military magistrates who were ignorant of the constitution of the merchant guild. In addition, the tribunal would lose its jurisdiction over merchants enrolled in the urban and provincial militia elsewhere in the viceroyalty. In a word, a literal interpretation of the viceregal order would be contrary to reason and precedent.[20]

The consulado's representation was followed by a new request for clarification from the *subdelegado* of Zinapécuaro. When the royal decree had been first published, he asserted, he had asked Viceroy Revillagigedo whether it conceded the civil *fuero* to enlisted militiamen. Revillagigedo's declaration of July 6, 1793, had decided in the negative. Did Branciforte's order, he queried, reverse that decision? He thought not and proposed to continue to exercise jurisdiction in civil actions against militiamen of the ranks.[21] Some two weeks later, Bernadino Bonavía, the *corregidor* of Mexico, raised a question. On frequent occasions, he reported, military personnel refused to recognize the right of civil authorities to arrest them for violations of police regulations. Bonavía desired to know whether soldiers, including personnel of the urban and provincial militia, were exempt from the observance of such regulations by virtue of the royal decree.[22]

The implications of Branciforte's order also disturbed the officials of the *Cuerpo de Minería,* the mining guild of New Spain. This corporation possessed jurisdiction in all litigation arising from the provisions of

its ordinances, including both private suits and official actions initiated
to enforce the ordinances. Jurisdiction was exercised, in the first
instance, by subordinate tribunals, called *diputaciones territoriales,*
which existed in the several mining districts. Within the Audiencia of
Mexico, initial appeals went to the *tribunal general,* the supreme
governing body of the guild, and second appeals to a specially
constituted court called a *juzgado de alzadas.* The latter was composed of a member of the audiencia designated by the viceroy, the
director-general of the general tribunal, and a third judge elected
by the general assembly of the guild. In the Audiencia of New
Galicia, both first and second appeals were heard by *juzgados de
alzadas* composed of a judge of that audiencia and two miners
selected every three years by the general assembly.[23]

In January, 1795, the general tribunal dispatched a lengthy protest to the viceroy. It conceded that the royal decree, by confirming
the private and exclusive competence of the military magistracy in
actions against soldiers, was intended to apply to both regulars and
militia. The tribunal maintained, however, that the enactment
operated only as against the ordinary jurisdiction and that it in no
way affected other privileged *fueros* such as that of the mining guild.
These were and continued to be just as private and just as exclusive
as the military. This principle, it asserted, was firmly established in
law. Branciforte, himself, had subscribed to it. On June 25, 1794,
he had determined that the royal decree in no way limited the
jurisdiction of the consulado, and on October 25, 1794, he had
declared that only mining courts could take cognizance of actions
against soldiers for violations of the mining ordinances, even though
those soldiers enjoyed the *fuero militar* in all its amplitude.[24]

The tribunal contended that if Branciforte's later order reversed
these precedents an intolerable situation would arise. The mining
ordinances, it pointed out, provided that title to a mine might be
denounced for abandonment of work or for inobservance of various
laws of the ordinances by the owner.[25] But suppose that a civilian
wanted to denounce a title belonging to an individual who enjoyed
the *fuero militar?* Or suppose that civilian miners undertook a
drainage operation benefiting a mine at a higher level which belonged
to a soldier, and suppose that the latter refused to pay a fair share of

the costs as provided by the ordinances?[26] Moreover, asked the tribunal, what about instances in which a soldier who was in partnership with civilian miners did not fulfill his obligations, or in which a soldier who owned a mine did not comply with the established standards of wages, work assignments, and methods of payment?[27] In addition, how about official actions against soldier miners for nonobservance of the ordinances?[28] In each case the aggrieved party would have to bring action before a military magistrate. This would mean that the enforcement of the mining ordinances would be in the hands of persons who were unfamiliar with the constitution of the community of miners instead of in those of justices, who by the terms of the ordinance, must have at least ten years of experience in the industry. Such a situation was contrary to the king's wishes and to all reason. It would lead to confusion, delay, and injustices in the administration of the law.[29]

Furthermore, continued the tribunal, as there were no military magistrates in many mining districts, it would be necessary to carry litigation to the captaincy general. By having to appear before a court far distant from their homes, parties to suits, whether they were soldiers or civilians, would be put to considerable expense and inconvenience. In cases of a minor nature which should be decided summarily, aggrieved persons would have to spend more than they would receive from a favorable judgment and so would simply waive their right to a hearing. Also, with no local authority to enforce the mining ordinances against soldiers, violations could be committed with impunity.

Thus, summarized the tribunal, if the military jurisdiction were allowed to intrude into affairs of the mining community, both civilian and soldier miners would be subjected to inconveniences, injustices, and financial loss. Moreover, the industry itself would be disrupted through ineffectual or improper administration of the ordinances which governed it. In this connection it was pointed out that the *aviadores* (financial backers of mining enterprisers) were cautious and suspicious men and that they would be much less likely to invest in an industry where jurisdiction was split and where litigation might be handled by magistrates who were not professionally competent. Such a situation would serve to discourage the capital investment which was so necessary to the health and progress of the industry. Finally, mining was such an important enterprise that if it were disrupted or depressed, the economy of the viceroyalty would suffer and the revenues derived by the royal treasury through taxes on production would be adversely affected. The tribunal concluded its representation by requesting that the mining jurisdiction be dispensed from the requirement of forwarding actions pending against soldiers to the captaincy general, that the private and exclusive character of its *fuero* be confirmed, and that in case there was any doubt in the mind of the viceroy about the validity of the tribunal's position, the entire question be referred to the crown.[30]

Branciforte sent the accumulated queries and representations to the *auditor de guerra* for an opinion. As an introduction to his reply, the *auditor* disposed of the basic issue in the controversy, namely, the purport of the royal decree of February 9, 1793. About this, he believed, there was no doubt. The enactment restored or confirmed to the military magistracy competence in all actions against soldiers with the two exceptions stated. Did it apply to the militia? The *auditor* thought it did, but only to the extent that it amplified the *fuero* this component already enjoyed. It did not concede the civil *fuero* to enlisted men.[31]

Turning to the claims of the tribunals of the consulado and the mining guild, the *auditor* denied that the privileged character of their two *fueros* conveyed any immunity from the universal application of the decree. This was clearly indicated by the use of the word "only" (*únicamente*) in establishing the two exceptions. Furthermore, and apparently in anticipation of just such arguments as employed by the two tribunals, the king had declared in the strongest and most categorical terms that by his own hand and by his royal authority all previous enactments which conflicted with the provisions of the decree were abrogated and annulled. Such a provision, according to established precedents, affected the special constitutions of the two guilds as well as general legislation.

The *auditor* scoffed at the claims of the consulado and the mining tribunal that special judges were necessary to administer the mercantile and mining codes. Many criminal actions against merchants, he pointed out, arose from violations of mercantile law and, according to the arguments of the consulado, a knowledge of the law merchant was necessary in order to dispose of them equitably. However, jurisdiction in such cases had been granted in a royal order of March 4, 1791, to the *Real Sala del Crimen,* whose ministers were not merchants. Other instances indicated that the crown did not consider it essential for merchants to judge mercantile cases. In Spain transient foreign merchants were subject in the second instance to the jurisdiction of the *Consejo Supremo de Guerra,* a body which most certainly was not made up of merchants.[32] In Mexico appeals from the decisions of the merchant and mining tribunals went to a *juzgado de alzadas.* In the latter court, a member of the audiencia presided and voted, although he was not a merchant. Moreover, argued the *auditor,* the mining and mercantile tribunals each possessed their *asesores* who in practice decided cases that came before the two courts. These officials were trained lawyers, not merchants or miners, and there was no reason to believe that they were any better qualified to hear commercial or mining cases than were the *asesores* and *auditores* who advised military judges. The *auditor* also expressed the opinion that the fears of the two tribunals were considerably exaggerated. After all, he pointed out, the numbers of miners and merchants who enjoyed the *fuero militar* in civil actions and who were thus exempt from their respective courts was negligible. In effect the mining and mercantile jurisdictions remained virtually intact despite the royal decree.

The *auditor* had little patience with the question raised by the *corregidor* of Mexico. That official certainly must be aware, he asserted, that the royal decree was not intended to exempt militiamen from the observance of police regulations or to pardon them for violations. It simply provided that they should be tried by military rather than by ordinary courts. In fact, the decree specifically stated that the penalties established by various regulations and enactments remained in full force.[33]

Viceroy Branciforte accepted the opinion of the *auditor* in its entirety, and on May 11, 1795, issued a declaration incorporating its main points. The militia was to continue to enjoy only the *fuero* it possessed before the publication of the royal decree of February 9, 1793; that is, the civil and criminal *fuero* for officers and the criminal *fuero* for enlisted men. When on active status, all ranks and grades enjoyed the complete *fuero militar*. For the militia, however, as for the regular army, all cases of *desafuero* were abolished except for the two mentioned in the decree. The declaration specifically confirmed the competence of the military jurisdiction in actions against soldiers in mining and mercantile law and in those arising from violations of police ordinances.[34]

Branciforte's action did not terminate the controversy. The consulado and the mining guild acknowledged the declaration but appealed to the crown.[35] Their efforts were successful. On March 20, 1797, a royal order declared that the viceroy's decision, insofar as it extended the *fuero militar* to cases in mining and mercantile law, was contrary to the laws of Castile and to the spirit and intent of the royal decree of February 9, 1793. Branciforte was therefore directed to restore the private and exclusive quality of the mining and mercantile *fueros*.[36] The viceroy suspended compliance until the crown made, as he put it, a "final" decision in the matter.[37] This tactic produced another royal order which repeated the earlier directions to the viceroy.[38] In the meantime, Branciforte was succeeded by Azanza and, in October, 1798, the new viceroy issued an order implementing the royal will.[39] Yet the controversy was not laid to rest. Azanza reported in 1799 that military and civil officials of the capital still did not agree on how the controversial decree affected the privileges of the militia.[40]

In summary, the increase of the Army of New Spain after the Seven Years' War resulted in a substantial extension of military privileges. The most important of these, the *fuero militar*, was frequently abused by its possessors and promoted numerous bitter and protracted disputes between civil and military authorities. As a consequence, the administration of justice was hampered, public order disturbed, and royal authority weakened. Civil officials and responsible military men recognized and deplored these evils. The general reorganization of the army begun in the late 1780's had, as one of its objectives, the reduction of military privileges and the curbing of their abuse. Such efforts were defeated by the need, real or fancied, for a larger military establishment, by the pretensions of the army, particularly the militia, and by the propensity for disputation exhibited by the military, the ordinary, and other privileged jurisdictions. Indeed, the evidence suggests strongly that after the reorganization disturbances arising from the *fuero militar*—and its abuse—grew in volume.[41] Nor did the end of Spanish dominion and the establishment of the republic solve the problem. On the contrary, the army, inherited from the viceroyalty, brought its privileges with it intact. Without the prestige and authority of the crown to limit their extreme abuse, these privileges became a powerful element in promoting praetorian government in Mexico.

Notes

(PAGES 77–82)

1. "Cumplim.ᵗᵒ a[1] R.¹ Decreto y ōrn̄ acompañatoria . . . ," AGN:IG 13 (1792–1794). The decree is reproduced in part in the *Novísima recopilación,* Lib. VI, tít. iv, ley 21.

2. See the comments of J. N. Rodríguez de San Miguel, *Pandectas hispano-megicanas,* II, note 2 to item 2121, p. 21.

3. *Bando,* May 22, 1793, "Cumplim.ᵗᵒ [al] R.¹ Decreto y ōrn̄ acompañatoria. . . ."

4. Verduga to Saavedra, México, May 29, 1793, *ibid.*

5. Saavedra to Verduga, México, (n.d.), and Saavedra to Revillagigedo, México, May 30, 1793, *ibid.*

6. Verduga to Revillagigedo, México, June 3, 1793, *ibid.*

7. Santa María to Rabago, México, June 17, 1793, *ibid.*

8. México, June 17, 1793, *ibid.*

9. Rabago to Revillagigedo, México, June 22, 1793, *ibid.*

10. Sánches to Días, Zinapécuaro, June 1, 1793, *ibid.*

11. Manuel Ramírez Arellano to Flon, Chicontepec [?], June 10, 1793, *ibid.*

12. Díaz to Revillagigedo, Valladolid, June 3, 1793, and Flon to Revillagigedo, Puebla, June 22, 1793, *ibid.*

13. Díaz de Salcedo to Revillagigedo, San Luis Potosí, June 21, 1793, *ibid.* Apparently the officers of the Legion had not yet lost their commissions as a result of Revillagigedo's disbandment of the provincial militia.

14. *Dictámenes,* June 3, and June 5, 1793, *ibid.*

15. *Dictamen,* June 10, 1793, *ibid.*

16. Circular order, México, July 6, 1793, *ibid.* I have taken the liberty to interpret Revillagigedo's order freely. Actually, it is not clear whether he meant that the decree affected the militia only in regard to the *fuero* which it already possessed or whether he meant that it did not affect it at all. The exact wording of the order is as follows: ". . . que el mencionado Real Decreto solo comprehende en toda su extension á los que sirven en Cuerpos Veteranos y á los que de esta clase se hallen en los de Milicias Provinciales y Urbanas, como Plazas de prest y continuo Servicio; pero todos los demas de dichas milicias mientras no estuvieren en actual Servicio, deben gozar unicamente el fuero concedido en Real Orden de 13 de Febrero de 1786. con arreglo á mi determinacion de 23 de Abril, y Reglamento provisional de 24 de Agosto de 1790. . . ."

17. *Ibid.*

18. November 16, 1794, "Recuerdo sobre el cumplim.ᵗᵒ del Real Decreto de 9 de Febrero de 93 . . . ," AGN:IG 13 (1792–1794).

19. November 28–30, 1794, *ibid.*

20. December 3, 1794, *ibid.*

21. Roque Sánches de Andrade to Phelipe Díaz de Hortega, Zinapécuaro, December 13, 1794, and Díaz de Hortega to Branciforte, Valladolid, December 15, 1794, *ibid.*

22. Bonavía to Branciforte, México, December 30, 1794, *ibid.*

23. *Reales ordenanzas para la dirección, régimen y gobierno del importante cuerpo de la minería de Nueva-España* . . . , Títs. II, III; Walter Howe, *The Mining Guild of New Spain and its Tribunal General, 1770–1821,* pp. 64–66, 268–269, 281–282.

24. México, January 16, 1795, "Recuerdo sobre el cumplim.ᵗᵒ del Real Decreto. . . ."

25. *Reales ordenanzas . . . de la minería de Nueva-España* . . . , Tít. VI, arts. 4–8, 11.

26. *Ibid.,* Tít. X, art. 16.

27. For example, the circumstances described in *ibid.,* Tít. XI, arts. 8–9, and Tít. XII, arts. 1, 8, 10.

28. *Ibid.,* Tít. IX, art. 10.

29. Mining Tribunal to Branciforte, México, January 16, 1795, "Recuerdo sobre el cumplim.ᵗᵒ del Real Decreto. . . ."

30. *Ibid.*

31. *Dictamen* of the *auditor,* México, March 17, 1795, *ibid.*

32. Cf. *Novísima recopilación,* Lib. VI, tít. xi, ley 5.

33. *Dictamen* of the *auditor,* México, March 17, 1795, "Recuerdo sobre el cumplim.ᵗᵒ del Real Decreto. . . ."

34. *Ibid.*

35. Royal order, March 20, 1797, *Gazeta de México,* IX (No. 14, Friday, November 17, 1798), 107.

36. *Ibid.,* pp. 107–108.

37. Branciforte to Alvarez, Orizaba, July 30, 1797, AGN:CV 4 (Branciforte, Reservada), no. 869.

38. May 16, 1798, *Gazeta de México,* IX (No. 14, Friday, November 17, 1798), 107.

39. October 20, 1798, AGN:B 19, no. 135.

40. Azanza to Alange, México, June 27, 1799, AGN:CV 6 (Azanza), no. 387.

41. This conclusion is based on the fact that I have encountered a great many more *expedientes* dealing with jurisdictional disputes dated after 1790 than before that year.

Appendices

APPENDIX ONE — Tables

APPENDIX TWO — Representative
Civil - Military Disputes

Appendix One

TABLE 1

THE ARMY OF NEW SPAIN, 1758[1]

REGULARS			
Infantry		*Cavalry*	
Battalion of the Crown (in Veracruz)	623	Company of the Vice-regal Guard	107
Company of the Vice-regal Guard	224	Flying squadrons of Nuevo León and Nuevo Santander	164
Halbardier Guard of the Viceroy	25		
Artillery		*Presidial Troops*	
Company of Veracruz	123	Isla del Carmen	162
		Acapulco	65
Dragoons		Pensacola	224
Corps of Veracruz	257	Northern Frontier	1,058
		Total Regulars	3,032

URBAN MILITIA[2]			
Infantry		*Cavalry*	
Regiment of Commerce of Mexico	---	Two companies of pork-butchers, bakers, and tanners of Mexico	---
Regiment of Commerce of Puebla	---		
Company of silver-smiths of Mexico	---	Company of pork-butchers, bakers, and tanners of Puebla	---
Corps of *pardos* of Mexico	---		

OTHER MILITIA UNITS[2]			
Lancers of Veracruz	---	Unorganized companies of infantry and cavalry of the coasts and the interior	---
Two infantry companies of *pardos* and *morenos* of Veracruz	---		

[1]Information compiled from "Estado que manifiesta el en que se hallan los Cuerpos de Infantería, Dragones, y Compañias Sueltas que hay en el Reino de Nueva España. . . ," México, September 7, 1758, AGN:CV 3 (Amarillas), fol. 419; "Instrucción del sr. conde de Revillagigedo al sr. marqués de las Amarillas," México, November 28, 1754, *Instrucciones que los vireyes de Nueva España dejaron a sus sucesores*, pars. 133–135, p. 28; "La organización del ejército en Nueva España," *Boletín del archivo general de la nación*, XI (October-November-December, 1940), pp. 622–632, 660–662.

[2,3]I have found no strengths for individual militia units or for the militia as a whole. In any case such figures would mean little because, as stated in Chapter I, most units were understrength and many existed in name only.

TABLE 2

THE ARMY OF NEW SPAIN, 1766[1]

REGULARS			
Infantry		*Dragoons*	
Regiment of America	1,671	Regiment of Spain	320
		Regiment of Mexico	240
	Artillery		
Company of Veracruz		110	
		Total Regulars	2,341[2]

PROVINCIAL MILITIA[3]			
Infantry		*Dragoons*	
Regiment of Mexico	1,000	Regiment of Puebla	638
Regiment of Tlaxcala	991		
Regiment of Puebla	991	*Cavalry*	
Regiment of Córdova	991	Regiment of Que-	
Regiment of Toluca	1,000	rétaro	648
Regiment of Veracruz	530	Lancers of Veracruz	714
Battalion of Oaxaca	465	Cadre of regulars	
Battalion of *pardos*		for the formation	
of Puebla	280	of a second cav-	
Battalion of *pardos*		alry regiment	38
of Mexico	520		
Two companies of			
pardos and *morenos*			
of Veracruz	438		
		Total Provincial Militia	9,244

[1]Adapted from "Estado en que se manifiesta el en que se hallan las Tropas . . . de se compone el Exercito . . . de la Nueva España," August 23, 1766, AGN:IG 236 (1766). The figures given, as was the contemporary practice, are for the enlisted strengths of line companies. They do not include company officers or the officers and men of the command and staff groups of regiments and battalions. No attempt is made here to detail the numbers of officers per unit or the strengths of command and staff groups, but I calculate that these elements would add approximately 6 per cent, or about 780 officers and men, to the grand total.

[2]The total for regulars does not include the troops stationed on the northern frontier or the garrisons of the Isla del Carmen and Acapulco. I have no figures for these elements, but they should not differ much from the strengths shown in Table 1.

[3]Provincial regiments and battalions contained cadres of regular officers and enlisted men to assist in training and stiffen discipline. For example, each company of both infantry and mounted regiments included one lieutenant and six noncommissioned officers who were regulars. In addition, certain key positions in command and staff groups were held by officers and men of the regular army (*Estado* of the Regiment of Provincial Infantry of Toluca, December 9, 1765, and *Estado* of the Regiment of Provincial Cavalry of Querétaro, December 10, 1765, AGN:RC 88, no. 77).

TABLE 2 (Cont.)

URBAN MILITIA

Infantry		*Cavalry*	
Regiment of Commerce of Mexico	908	Companies of bakers, pork-butchers, and tanners of Mexico	200
Regiment of Commerce of Puebla	246		
Company of silver-smiths of Mexico	100		

Total Urban Militia 1,454

Grand Total 13,039

TABLE 3

THE ARMY OF NEW SPAIN, 1784[1]

REGULARS

Infantry		*Dragoons*	
Regiment of Zamora	1,377	Regiment of Spain	522
Regiment of the Crown	1,377	Regiment of Mexico	522
Two fixed companies of San Juan de Ulúa	240	*Artillery*	
Fixed Company of Acapulco	105	Two companies	246

Total Regulars 4,389[2]

PROVINCIAL MILITIA

Infantry		*Dragoons*	
Regiment of Mexico	1,464	Regiment of Puebla	588
Regiment of Tlaxcala and Puebla	1,464	Regiment of Valladolid (Michoacán)	588
Regiment of Córdova and Jalapa	1,464		
Regiment of Toluca	1,464		
Battalion of Oaxaca	758		

[1]Adapted from *Estado* of the Army of New Spain, Crespo, "Dictamen," Quaderno 8. There are unexplained discrepancies between the unit strengths given by Crespo in his *estado* and the strengths of these units as shown in the individual tables of organization which I have examined. It is my opinion that in the case of regular units, his strengths are for enlisted personnel only, including those in the command and staff groups. In regard to the provincial militia, his figures appear to be for enlisted militiamen, including supernumeraries assigned to each company, but excluding enlisted men of the regular cadre.

[2]The Crespo *estado* does not include regulars stationed in the Commandancy-General of the Provincias Internas. Because of their remoteness and the fact that they were under a separate command, these troops were not considered as part of the Army of New Spain proper.

TABLE 3 (cont.)

PROVINCIAL MILITIA (Cont.)			
Battalion of Valladolid	732	*Cavalry*	
Infantry of the *Legión*		Regiment of Querétaro	588
del *Príncipe*[3]	758	Lancers of Veracruz	400
Infantry of the *Legión*		Cavalry of the *Legión*	
de *San Carlos*[4]	928	del *Principe*	1,446
Battalion of *pardos* of		Cavalry of the *Legión*	
Mexico	758	de *San Carlos*	2,597
Battalion of *pardos* of			
Puebla	758		
		Total Provincial Militia	16,755

URBAN MILITIA			
Infantry		*Cavalry*	
Regiment of Commerce		Guild companies	
of Mexico	810	of Mexico	128
Regiment of Commerce			
of Puebla	328		
Company of silversmiths			
of Mexico	79		
Two companies of whites			
of Veracruz	226		
Two companies of			
pardos and *morenos*			
of Veracruz	270		
		Total Urban Militia	1,841

UNORGANIZED MILITIA OF THE GULF AND CARIBBEAN COASTS			
Infantry		*Cavalry*	
Battalion of San Blas	766	Eighty-three separate	
Eighty-two separate		companies	3,699
companies	5,218		
		Total Unorganized Militia	9,683

VARIOUS NEW AND OLD MILITIA UNITS OF UNDETERMINED CATEGORY			
Infantry		*Cavalry*	
Regiment of Guadalajara	1,557	Forty-seven separate	
Eighteen separate		companies	3,433
companies	1,448		
		Total	6,438
		Grand Total	39,106

[3,4]The *Legión del Príncipe* and the *Legión de San Carlos* were mixed units of infantry and cavalry. They were both raised by José de Gálvez in 1767, the first in the province of Guanajuato and the second in San Luis Potosí (Herbert Ingram Priestley, *José de Gálvez*, pp. 216–225).

TABLE 4

THE PROVINCIAL MILITIA AS PROPOSED BY CRESPO[1]

Units	PEACE			WAR		
		Cavalry and			Cavalry and	
Infantry	Infantry	Dragoons	Total	Infantry	Dragoons	Total
Regiment of Mexico	833		833	1,361		1,361
Regiment of Tlaxcala	833		833	1,361		1,361
Regiment of Córdova	833		833	1,361		1,361
Regiment of Toluca	833		833	1,361		1,361
Battalion of Guanajuato	417		417	681		681
Battalion of San Carlos (District of San Luis Potosí)	417		417	680		680
Battalion of Oaxaca	417		417	681		681
Battalion of Valladolid	417		417	680		680
Battalion of *pardos* of Mexico	417		417	681		681
Battalion of *pardos* of Puebla	417		417	680		680
Elite Corps of Grenadiers	1,139		1,139	1,139		1,139
Elite Corps of *Cazadores*	1,139		1,139	1,139		1,139
Cavalry and Dragoons						
Regiment of Cavalry of Querétaro		361	361		613	613
Regiment of Cavalry of the Prince (District of Guanajuato)		361	361		613	613
Regiment of Cavalry of San Carlos (District of San Luis Potosí)		361	361		613	613
Regiment of Cavalry of San Luis (District of San Luis Potosí)		361	361		613	613
Regiment of Dragoons of Puebla		361	361		617	617
Regiment of Dragoons of Valladolid		361	361		617	617
Elite Corps of Volunteer Dragoons		617	617		617	617
Lancers of Veracruz		180	180		306	306
Totals	8,112	2,963	11,075	11,805	4,609	16,414

[1]Adapted from "Resumen general de fuerzas . . . que se proponen . . . ," Crespo, "Dictamen," Quaderno 2, Resumen 29.

TABLE 5

THE ARMY OF NEW SPAIN, 1800[1]

REGULARS[2]			
Infantry		*Cavalry*	
Regiment of the Crown	979	Flying Company of Nuevo	
Regiment of Spain	979	León	100
Regiment of Mexico[3]	979	Flying companies of Nuevo	
Regiment of Puebla[4]	979	Santander	225
Battalion of Veracruz	502		
Two light companies			
of Catalonia	160		
Dragoons		*Presidial Troops*	
Regiment of Spain	461	Fixed companies of the	
Regiment of Mexico	461	Isla del Carmen	143
		Fixed Company of Acapulco	77
		Fixed Company of San Blas	105
		Total Regulars	6,150

PROVINCIAL MILITIA			
Infantry		*Dragoons*	
Regiment of Mexico	845	Regiment of Puebla	367
Regiment of Toluca	845	Regiment of Michoacán	367
Regiment of Tlaxcala	845	Regiment of the Queen	367
Regiment of Puebla	845	Regiment of New Galicia	367
Regiment of Córdova,		Regiment of San Luis	367
Orizaba, and Jalapa	845	Regiment of San Carlos	367
Regiment of Valladolid	845		
Regiment of Celaya	845	*Cavalry*	
Battalion of Oaxaca	423	Regiment of Querétaro	367
Battalion of Guadalajara	423	Regiment of the Prince	367
Battalion of Guanajuato	423	Lancers of Veracruz	1,000
Two companies of *pardos*			
and *morenos* of Veracruz	210		
		Total Provincial Militia	11,330

[1]Adapted from "Noticia que manifiesta el número de tropas de que constan los Cuerpos Provinciales y Urbanos y demás Milicias del Reyno de N.E. con algunas veteranas fixas . . . ," México, March 27, 1800, AGN:IG 386 (1793–1817). Figures given for units and divisions are for total enlisted strengths. In the case of the provincial units they apparently include the regular cadres.

[2]The "Noticia" does not include the garrisons of the Provincias Internas (except for the provinces of Nuevo León and Nuevo Santander which were directly dependent on the viceroyalty). These troops, as indicated in Table 3, were not considered as part of the Army of New Spain proper. Neither does it include three companies of artillery of 125 men each (*El viagero universal*, XXVI, 322).

[3,4]These two regiments were temporarily stationed in Havana ("Instrucción del señor Marquina al señor Iturrigaray," Tacubaya, January 1, 1803, *Instrucciones que los vireyes de Nueva España dejaron a sus sucesores,* par. 153, p. 183).

TABLE 5 (cont.)

METROPOLITAN URBAN MILITIA		
Regiment of Commerce of Mexico	702	
Battalion of Commerce of Puebla	228	
Squadron of Guild Cavalry of Mexico	129	
	Total Metropolitan Urban Militia	1,059

COASTAL MILITIA				
1st Division, Gulf Coast	400	1st Division, Pacific Coast	680	
2nd Division, Gulf Coast	670	2nd Division, Pacific Coast	774	
3rd Division, Gulf Coast	789	3rd Division, Pacific Coast	250	
4th Division, Gulf Coast	600	4th Division, Pacific Coast	300	
Companies of Tabasco	910	5th Division, Pacific Coast	450	
Isla del Carmen	300	6th Division, Pacific Coast	580	
		7th Division, Pacific Coast	400	
		Total Coastal Militia		7,103

FRONTIER MILITIA				
Corps of Colotlán	720	Companies of Nuevo		
Corps of Sierra Gorda	240	León	2,000	
Corps of Nuevo		Companies of Nuevo		
Santander	360	Santander	1,000	
		Total Frontier Militia		4,320

REPLACEMENT MILITIA[5]		
	Grand Total	29,962

[5]The replacement militia of the intendancies of Mexico, Puebla, Oaxaca, and Guadalajara are listed in the "Noticia," but no strengths are given. However, an earlier report by Viceroy Branciforte shows 4,306 men in the replacement companies of Mexico, Puebla, Oaxaca, Guadalajara, and Valladolid ("Exército de Nueva España. Resumen general de sus fuerzas . . . ," accompanying Inc. No. 6 to "Instrucción del virey marqués de Branciforte a su sucesor don Miguel José de Azanza," Orizaba, March 16, 1797, *Instrucciones que los vireyes de Nueva España dejaron a sus sucesores,* following p. 148).

Appendix Two

FOLLOWING are abstracts of representative disputes involving the military and the ordinary jurisdictions which supplement the material in the text. In certain instances where *expedientes* from which abstracts were drawn are incomplete or where testimony is not clear, I have taken the liberty of rounding out the accounts in a manner indicated by the material that is available. Such interpolations, however, relate to details and do not affect the basic issues.

A[1]*

IN THE Villa of Salamanca, on the morning of May 29, 1796, Francisco Grande, sublieutenant of the third company of the Regiment of Provincial Infantry of Celaya, called at the residence of Manuel Martínez de Alegre, acting *alcalde,* to protest that Martínez had arrested one of his servants without informing him.[2] In the course of the ensuing discussion tempers rose. Martínez became very upset and, charging that Grande was showing disrespect to the office of *alcalde,* ordered the militia officer arrested and confined in the public jail. To carry out this order the *alcalde* and some of his associates who were present apparently laid hands on Grande. Since the day was Sunday, the company had gathered for weekly drill and one of the non-commissioned officers, who was informed of the altercation reported it to the acting company commander, Lieutenant Félix María Colón de Larreátegui. Colón immediately donned his uniform and hurried to the house of the *alcalde.* There he accused Martínez in the strongest terms of exceeding his jurisdiction and demanded that Grande be released. The *alcalde,* using equally positive language, refused. A bitter dispute developed and finally Colón called on one of his men who was present to muster the company and bring it to the scene. Martínez responded by ordering the *alguacil mayor* to gather a force of armed citizens to support him.

As word of the quarrel spread a crowd of civilians and militiamen gathered before the house of the *alcalde.* Both factions were in an ugly mood, and another officer of the company, fearing a riot, implored Colón to leave. The latter finally agreed to do so, but insisted on taking Grande with him. With the departure of Colón the crowd dispersed and the danger of violence was averted. Lieutenant Colón subsequently reported the incident to the regimental commander who in turn forwarded a complaint to the viceroy that the military jurisdiction had been invaded. Martínez, on his part, dispatched a justification of his conduct through civil channels. Upon receiving the rival accounts, Branciforte ordered that an impartial investigation be conducted and that, in view of the great scandal the affair had created in Salamanca, the guilty party be punished publicly. Unfortunately the *expediente* ends at this point and the final outcome of the dispute cannot be given.

B[3]

THIS CONTROVERSY involved as the principal parties the justice of the jurisdiction of Ometepec, Juan Francisco Perales; the commandant of the Fourth Division of Militia of the Pacific Coast, Captain José Ygnacio Flury; and the latter's adjutant, Lieutenant Antonio Junco. It grew out of several

*Appendix notes are on page 106.

100

incidents. Late in November, 1794, Perales attempted to apprehend militiaman Vicente Montezuma (alias Huescas), allegedly a minor who had run away from his father, in order to return him to the *patria potestad.* Montezuma declined arrest on the grounds of his military *fuero* but subsequently the justice was able to apprehend him. Upon hearing of Perales' action, Montezuma's company commander requested that the prisoner be remanded to military custody. The justice refused, whereupon the captain sought the assistance of Lieutenant Junco. Although the appeal arrived late at night, Junco arose from his bed, called on Perales, and seconded the request. After an extended argument, Perales agreed, apparently with the understanding that the next day Montezuma would be released to the ordinary jurisdiction so that he could be sent back to his father. As it happened, however, Junco refused to make the release on the grounds that Perales' procedure in the apprehension of the prisoner had violated the military jurisdiction. Furthermore, he maintained that the justice, by sending Montezuma back to his father, was making himself an accomplice in the crime of desertion.

A few days later a second incident occurred. On the night of November 30 a police patrol confiscated the machete of Francisco Vergara, another militiaman of Ometepec, for reasons that from the testimony are not clear. Vergara complained to his captain, who in turn appealed to Junco. The latter requested Perales to return the weapon because Vergara needed it in his work. The justice insisted that he had acted within his powers and refused to comply. At this juncture Commandant Flury arrived in Ometepec to inspect the militia company and was informed by Junco of the difficulties with Perales. Flury supported the position of his adjutant. In the case of Vergara's machete he demanded that it be returned or that Perales show cause for its confiscation. In the matter of Montezuma's arrest, Flury informed Perales that although the *Real declaración de milicias provinciales* authorized civil judges to arrest militiamen, it also required that the nearest officer or noncommissioned officer be notified immediately of the arrest and the reason for it. It provided, furthermore, that the colonel or commandant be supplied with copies of the charges within twenty-four hours so that he could determine whether the case was covered by the *fuero militar.*[4] Perales apparently had not complied with these provisions.

Flury himself precipitated a third incident. Upon the complaint of militiaman Manuel Joseph that four animals belonging to Dionisio Moreno had damaged his crops, the commandant assessed Moreno four pesos damages and impounded the animals until the money was paid. It was now Perales' turn to protest. He charged that the ordinary jurisdiction was being invaded and demanded that the animals be returned to their owner and that Joseph's complaints be handled through the customary civil channels.

In this impasse Flury and Perales appealed to higher authority. The former in a strongly worded letter to Branciforte, claimed that Perales was not only guilty of a technical offense in violating the military *fuero* but that he was also persecuting the militiamen of Ometepec and disturbing the peace. Furthermore, he added, the situation in Ometepec was not unique. Throughout the district comprising his command, the ordinary justices oppressed the militiamen and ignored the provisions of the *Real declaración de milicias provinciales* as well as the royal decree of February 9, 1793. Perales wrote to the Intendant of Puebla complaining that the arbitrary actions of the military authorities stirred up dissension within the community and destroyed respect for royal authority. He requested the intendant to ask the viceroy for orders directing Flury and Junco to cease their interference in cases where competence properly belonged to the ordinary courts. The arguments of the disputants were submitted to the *auditor de guerra,* who on January 12, 1795, issued a decision. Both parties, he pronounced, were at fault. Flury had invaded the ordinary jurisdiction by impounding the stock of Moreno. On the other hand, Perales had violated the *fuero militar* by confiscating the machete of Vergara and in his illegal procedure in the arrest and confinement of Montezuma. He recommended, therefore, that the viceroy order the machete and stock returned to their owners and that Flury and Perales be enjoined to confine themselves to their respective jurisdictions in the future. Branciforte accepted the opinion of the *auditor* and issued the appropriate orders.

C[5]

THE FOLLOWING INCIDENT is rather unusual in that a soldier is seeking the protection of an ordinary justice against the authority of a military magistrate.

Sometime in November, 1798, María de la Luz (alias "la Cupido") appeared before Manuel de Flon, the Governor-Intendant of Puebla, charging that José Miguel Cortés, a soldier of the Regiment of Commerce of Puebla, had mistreated her. Flon summoned the soldier, and when the latter confessed to the charge, he ordered him in overnight barracks arrest. Cortés, however, apparently did not report for confinement and instead appealed to the junior *alcalde ordinario* of the city, Nicolás Rosales. The *alcalde* thereupon issued a strongly worded writ to the governor challenging the latter's authority and ordering that Cortés be left at liberty.[6] During the next two weeks a heated exchange of correspondence took place between Flon and Rosales in the course of which the latter supported his actions with a written opinion of his *asesor,* Manuel de Mena. As a result of the imbroglio, Flon directed an outraged protest to the viceroy. "Since the conquest of this kingdom," he fumed, "never has a military governor been so insulted as I. . . . never since there have been armies has there been an example such as this." If, he stated, Rosales had simply wanted to present a protest or to report circumstances in the case of which Flon was not aware, his communication would have received every consideration. Instead, he had dispatched a document full of demands, threats, and incitements to *competencias* so that, as Flon declared, ". . . it was necessary for me to exert all my self-control to prevent myself from administering military punishment [to the *alcalde*] for his insolence." The governor acknowledged that the case of Luz *v.* Cortés was unimportant in itself; it was the private and exclusive character of the military jurisdiction which he exercised that was at stake.

Flon's protest was submitted to the *fiscal de lo civil* of the Audiencia of Mexico for an opinion. The latter official declared that Rosales had most certainly exceeded his authority by issuing demands to a military governor in an action where the accused so obviously was of the *fuero militar.* If the *alcalde* felt that he should intervene in the case, he simply should have sent his testimony to the governor so that the latter might take it into consideration. In order, therefore, to provide Flon with public satisfaction and the vindication of his authority which he sought, the *fiscal* recommended that Rosales be fined fifty pesos and an equal fine be levied against the *asesor,* Manuel de Mena, for providing the *alcalde* with unsound counsel. In addition, Rosales should be warned to seek more competent legal advice in the future and Mena should be enjoined to familiarize himself with the law. The case was next passed to the viceroy's *asesor general,* who, in general, agreed with the *fiscal.*[7] He felt, however, that since the real source of trouble was Mena's advice, the latter should be fined but the *alcalde* dismissed with the warning recommended by the *fiscal.* Viceroy Azanza agreed with the *asesor general,* and on December 21, 1798, issued the appropriate decree.

D[8]

ON MAY 7, 1787, Miguel Saens de Sicilia, appeared before Pedro Anteparaluceta, acting *corregidor* of Coyoacán, to lodge a complaint against the hacienda of Coapa [Quapa, Quapam], a property which belonged to the estate of the late colonel of militia, the Conde de Torre Cosío. Saens charged that the operators of Coapa had diverted a stream which normally ran through that property into a channel cutting through his own hacienda of San Juan de Dios. As a result his land had been flooded and his crops damaged. The plaintiff petitioned that Anteparaluceta order the operators of Coapa to restore the stream to its original course. Upon investigation, the *corregidor* found that the situation was as Saens had claimed and ordered the restoration. This was accomplished. Shortly thereafter, however, Saens reported to Anteparaluceta that the stream had again been diverted onto his hacienda, and the *corregidor* once more ordered that it be returned to its old course. Again this was done, but a short time later Saens charged that the stream had been rediverted. Anteparaluceta took the administrator and the major-domo of Coapa sharply to task. Both testified that they were acting under the direct orders of Esteban González de Cosío, agent of the widowed countess and captain in the Regiment of Provincial Infantry of Toluca. Therefore, they stated, they could not be held responsible. The *corregidor,* nevertheless, arrested them and, in addition, wrote to the viceroy charging that González de Cosío had disregarded and mocked the royal jurisdiction.

Upon the arrest of her employees, the countess lodged a complaint against Anteparaluceta in the *Juzgado del Estado y Marquesado del Valle.* That tribunal supported the actions of the *corregidor.* In a decision issued on July 4, 1787, it ordered the operators of Coapa to maintain the stream in its original channel and assessed costs against the countess. Anteparaluceta, however, was directed to release the prisoners with an appropriate warning. The countess appealed to the Audiencia of Mexico, which on July 27 upheld the decision of the lower court. At that time no action was taken on the complaint of the *corregidor* about the jurisdictional aspects of the case. Then, three years later and under circumstances not stated, the *auditor de guerra* finally directed his attention to the question. On July 6, 1790, he offered the opinion that Anteparaluceta had no grounds for complaint. Because both the late count and González de Cosío possessed the complete *fuero militar,* the *corregidor* had no jurisdiction and Saens should have lodged his charges with the military magistracy. On the other hand, had this been done, the *auditor* had no doubt that the captaincy general would have decided the case in the same manner as the civil tribunals. He therefore recommended that the viceroy deny the competence of Anteparaluceta, but as captain general confirm the decision of the audiencia. Revillagigedo accepted the opinion of the *auditor,* and on July 8 issued the appropriate orders.

E[9]

ON JUNE 11, 1796, the *subdelegado* of Ameca, Ignacio de Herrera, sent to the viceroy the records of actions initiated by the ordinary jurisdiction since 1791 against José Antonio Aguilar (alias Greñas), a soldier of the Regiment of Provincial Infantry of Tlaxcala. In the covering letter he charged that Aguilar was a depraved and habitual criminal and that he was insubordinate and disrespectful to royal justices. More specifically, he had carried and had used deadly weapons against peaceful citizens; he was responsible for creating riots and disturbances, and he had posted publicly in Ozumba lewd and insolent pasquinades against Herrera's predecessor. The *subdelegado*, moreover, stated that Aguilar before enlisting had been twice convicted for criminal offenses and was, therefore, unfit for militia service. Although as a militiaman he enjoyed the criminal *fuero*, his disrespect and resistance to royal justices clearly constituted cases of *desafuero*. Nevertheless, continued Herrera, his company commander, Vicente Ruiz Bustamante, had refused to cooperate in his arrest. The *subdelegado* reported that on the preceding March 25 his agents finally were able to apprehend Aguilar, but on the same day he escaped with the assistance of Miguel Rodríguez, a militiaman of the same company, and fled to Tlaxcala where he claimed the protection of his regimental officers. Herrera requested the viceroy to order the culprit returned to his jurisdiction for trial.

Meanwhile, on the same day that Aguilar was apprehended and escaped, Herrera arrested Rodríguez, apparently on the charge that, by assisting Aguilar, he had resisted a royal justice in the performance of his duty. Captain Ruiz demanded that Rodríguez be remanded to his custody since the prisoner enjoyed the criminal *fuero*. The *subdelegado* refused. The offense, he maintained, was a case of *desafuero* and Rodríguez should be punished so that militiamen would learn to respect royal justices. The implication was that this end would not be accomplished if the case were handled by the military. At this juncture the sergeant major of the second battalion of the regiment intervened to complain that Herrera was exceeding his jurisdiction and to demand that the records of the case against Rodríguez be forwarded to him. Again, the *subdelegado* refused and requested the viceroy for a decision. The sergeant major appealed to the same authority. It was undeniable, he declared, that resistance to a royal justice was indeed a serious offense. On the other hand, the resistance, to be culpable, must be offered to a person who is actually invested with royal authority. There were grave doubts in his mind whether the agents of Herrera who had arrested Aguilar possessed any such authority and, therefore, whether Rodríguez had been guilty of resistance in a technical sense when he assisted the former to escape.

The *auditor de guerra* issued separate decisions on the two *competencias*. In the case of Aguilar, he declared that the militiaman had been guilty of serious crimes and was unfit for the glorious profession of arms. Furthermore, he was under the minimum height required for militia service. The *auditor*, therefore, recommended that the culprit be separated from the service and turned over to the ordinary jurisdiction for prosecution. In the case of Rodríguez, the *auditor* declared that the *subdelegado* should have submitted the records to the sergeant major as requested, but that the latter should not depreciate the nature of the crime. Since the testimony indicated the guilt of the accused, it was recommended that Captain Ruiz place Rodríguez in arrest for eight days and that the latter be cautioned that if he repeated his offense he would be punished severely. The viceroy accepted the opinions of the *auditor* and on July 21 and 22, 1796, issued the appropriate orders.

F[10]

ON JULY 10, 1791, Ambrosio del Valle, a lieutenant of the *Acordada*, arrested Diego Fernández Nieto, a corporal in the militia of Orizaba, for complicity in a homicide. The captain of the company informed the colonel of the regiment of the arrest. The latter, judging that the case was not one of *desafuero*, requested Valle to turn the prisoner and the records of the case over to him as provided by the *Real declaración de milicias provinciales*. Valle refused on grounds that the nature of the case was not clear and that he was not certain whether it pertained to the military jurisdiction. The colonel appealed to the inspector general who, citing the appropriate articles of the *Real declaración*, upheld the regimental commander.[11] If, added the inspector, Valle knew that the culprit was a militiaman he should have sought authority for the arrest from the military, thus preventing quarrels, and injuries to the *fuero militar* which inevitably resulted when ordinary justices acted without a proper knowledge of the limits of their authority. After investigating the dispute, the *auditor de guerra* recommended that the prisoner be turned over to the military jurisdiction for trial and on August 21, 1791, the viceroy so ordered. On December 18, 1792, Nieto was sentenced to the Presidio of San Juan de Ulúa.

G[12]

IN MEXICO, on the night of December 7, 1803, a young negro slave, José Miguel de la O, ran away from his master, Lieutenant Manuel Gilabert of the Regiment of Infantry of Puebla, and sought refuge in the house of *Alcalde* Manuel de Cuebas y Luyando. José Miguel complained that he had been treated with cruelty and asked for a license to seek a new master. Gilabert demanded his property back. The lad, he testified, was valuable. Moreover, he had spent considerable time and effort teaching him Christian doctrine and preparing him for a useful life. Unfortunately, José Miguel had come under the influence of a common woman of the streets and her children and, using as an excuse the punishment he had received for not knowing his lesson, had fled. Gilabert maintained that the lad was only fourteen years old and as a minor was not legally competent to seek a new owner. The lieutenant also claimed that both he and the slave possessed the *fuero militar* and that the *alcalde* had no jurisdiction in the matter. Cuebas, however, refused to relinquish custody of José Miguel on the grounds that he was the official protector of minors and that he did not feel the case came under the *fuero militar*. The dispute was submitted to the *auditor de guerra* who declared that inasmuch as Gilabert so obviously enjoyed the military *fuero*, the *alcalde* had no jurisdiction over the slave or his master. He, therefore, recommended that José Miguel be returned to Gilabert and that if Cuebas wished to pursue the matter further, he should make his representations to the captaincy general. Viceroy Iturrigaray agreed with the *auditor* and issued the appropriate order.

Notes

1. Abstracted from "Regimiento Provincial de Infanteria de Celaya. . . . Contra Don Manuel Martinez de Alegre por haber este mandado amarrar al Sub.^te . . . D. Fran.^co Grande . . . ," AGN:IG 155 (1782–1796).

2. The reason for the arrest is not clear from the testimony.

3. Abstracted from "El Comand.^te de la 4.ª Division de Milicias de la Costa del Sur, y el Justicia de Ometepec sobre excesos por ambas jurisdicciones," AGN:IG 289 (1795–1797).

4. Tít. VIII, art. 20.

5. Abstracted from "El. Gov.^or intend.^te de Puebla informa con docum.^tos el motivo de la prision del Soldado del Comercio d.^n Mig.^l Cortés . . . ," AGN:IG 171 (1797–1799).

6. The circumstances of Rosales' intervention in the case are not clear. The correspondence of that official with Flon is missing from the *expediente,* but other documents in the case suggest that at the time of Cortés' arrest by the governor some action involving Cortés and María de la Luz was pending before the ordinary magistrate.

7. This official was apparently performing the functions of an *auditor de guerra.*

8. Abstracted from "Queja del Correg.^or de Cuyoacan, contra el Cap.^n de Miliz.^as de Toluca d.^n Esteban Gonzalez de Cosio, sobre haver bulner.^do la jurisd.^n R.^l," AGN:IG 103 (1790–1794).

9. Abstracted from "Expedientes sobre dificultades entre autoridades civiles y militares," AGN:IG 171 (1788–1796).

10. Abstracted from "Dilig.^s entre el Cap.^n de milicias de Orizava D. Marcos Gonz y un Ten.^e de la Acordada sͬeͫ la prision de un cabo . . . ," AGN:IG 160 (1780–1792).

11. The articles involved were 20 and 21 of Tít. VIII.

12. Abstracted from "Quexa de Dn Manuel Gilabert, Teniente del Regim.^to de Infant.^a de Puebla, contra el Alc.^e ordinario de esta Cuidad [*sic*] Dn Manuel Luyando, por un Negro Esclabo," AGN:IG 71 (1803–1810).

Bibliography

MANUSCRIPT MATERIAL

THIS STUDY is based largely on manuscript sources in Mexican archives. Of this material the following items and *expedientes* are considered to be the most important:

Archivo General de la Nación, México (AGN)

Correspondencia de los Virreyes (CV)

"Estado que manifiesta el en que se hallan los Cuerpos de Infanteria, Dragones, y Compañias Sueltas que hay en el Reino de Nueva España. . . ." México, September 7, 1758. Vol. 3(Amarillas), fol. 419.

Viceroy the Conde de Revillagigedo to Secretary of State and the General War Office, the Conde del Campo de Alange. México, February 6, 1790. Vol. 22 (Revillagigedo, Reservada), no. 296.

Viceroy the Marqués de Branciforte to Secretary of State and the General War Office, the Conde del Campo de Alange. México, October 5, 1794. Vol. 1 (Branciforte, Reservada), no. 81.

Viceroy the Marqués de Cruillas to Minister of the Indies Julián de Arriaga. México, March 19, 1763. Vol. 10, no. 935.

Indiferente de Guerra (IG)

"El Comand.te de la 4.ª Division de Milicias de la Costa del Sur, y el Justicia de Ometepec sobre excesos por ambas jurisdicciones." 1795. Vol. 289 (1795-1797).

"Copias sobre el Costo de las milicias del Reyno, y su mal estado." September, 1780. Vol. 65A (1718–1780).

"Cumplim.to a[1] R.l Decreto y ōrn acompañatoria cortando disputas, y q.e los jueces militares conozcan de las causas civiles y criminales de sus individuos." 1793. Vol. 13 (1792–1794).

"Dilig.ˢ entre el Cap.ⁿ de milicias de Orizava D. Marcos Gōnz y un Ten.ᵉ de la Acordada s̄r̄e la prision de un cabo, nombrado Diego Fer̄n̄z Nieto." 1791. Vol. 160 (1780–1792).

"Estado en que manifiesta el en que se hallan las Tropas . . . de se compone el Exercito . . . de la Nueva España." August 23, 1766. Vol. 236 (1766).

"Expedientes sobre dificultades entre autoridades civiles y militares." 1796. Vol. 171 (1788–1796).

"Expediente sobre incidente entre el Real Tribunal del Consulado y el Regimiento del Comercio de Mexico." [1782–1786]. Vol. 122 (1783–1894 [sic]).

"Fuero Militar al Regim.to de Milicias Urbanas de esta Ciudad." December, 1773. Vol. 47 (1773–1775).

107

"El Gov.^{or} intend.^{te} de Puebla informa con docum.^{tos} el motivo de la prision del Soldado del Comercio d.^{n} Mig.^{1} Cortés. . . ." 1798. Vol. 171 (1797–1799).

"Noticia que manifiesta el numero de tropas de que constan los Cuerpos Provinciales y Urbanos y demas Milicias del Reyno de N. E. con algunas veteranas fixas. . . ." México, March 27, 1800. Vol. 386 (1793–1817).

"Nueva idea para formar Cuerpos Provinciales en el Reino, Luz para que se mejoren los ya establecidos, y varias reflecciones sobre el Servicio de Milicias. . . . [by] El Aiudante Maior del Regimiento de Dragones Provinciales de Michoacan, Don Manuel Antonio de Mora." Valladolid, May 25, 1784. Vol. 14 (1784–1785).

"Queja del Correg.^{or} de Cuyoacan, contra el Cap.^{n} de Miliz.^{as} de Toluca d.^{n} Esteban Gonzalez de Cosio, sobre haver bulner.^{do} la jurisd.^{n} R.^{l}" 1790. Vol. 103 (1790–1794).

"Quexa de Dn Manuel Gilabert, Teniente del Regim.^{to} de Infant.^{a} de Puebla, contra el Alc.^{e} ordinario de esta Cuidad [sic] Dn Manuel Luyando, por un Negro Esclabo." 1803. Vol. 71 (1803–1810).

"Recuerdo sobre el cumplim.^{to} del Real Decreto de 9 de Febrero de 93 acerca del Fuero militar." 1794. Vol. 13 (1792–1794).

"Regimiento Provincial de Infanteria de Celaya. Tercera Compañia. Criminal. Contra Don Manuel Martinez de Alegre por haber este mandado amarrar al sub.^{te} de la misma compañia D. Fran.^{co} Grande. . . ." Salamanca, 1796. Vol. 155 (1782–1796).

"Reglamento Provicional de Milicias de Villa de Cordoba y Xalapa. . . ." México, January 14, 1775. Vol. 51 (1773–1775). This item is reproduced in "El ejército de Nueva España a fines del siglo XVIII," Boletín del archivo general de la nación, IX (April-May-June, 1938), 240–269.

"Sobre dar nueba forma al Regimiento Urbano del Comercio de Mexico." 1791. Vol. 122 (1783–1894 [sic]).

"Testim.^{o} de los autos principales formados sobre averiguar el perjuicio, q.^{e} se causa á la R.^{l} Haz.^{a} en el Ramo de Tributos por el establecim.^{to} de Milicias. . . ." 1772. Vol. 252 (1772).

"Testim.^{o} del Quad.^{no} de autos formados sobre Testamentos de los Militares. . . ." 1772. Vol. 252 (1772).

Reales Cédulas (RC)

Royal order authorizing the reorganization of the militia of New Spain according to the plan of Inspector General Francisco Antonio Crespo. San Lorenzo, October 20, 1788. Vol. 141, no. 106. This item is reproduced in María del Carmen Velázquez, El estado de guerra en Nueva España, 1760–1808 (México, 1950), pp. 243–245.

Royal instructions to Lieutenant General Juan de Villalba y Angulo. San Ildefonso, August 1, 1764. Vol. 85, no. 142.

Biblioteca Nacional de México

"Dictamen del Coronel Dn Fran.^{co} Antonio Crespo, Inspector interino de las tropas del Virreynato de N.^{a} Esp.^{a} sobre su mejor arreglo y extablecim.^{to}," México, July 31, 1784. MS. 173.

PRINTED MATERIALS

LEGISLATIVE MATERIAL AND OFFICIAL DOCUMENTS

Bando conceding the *fuero militar* to the provincial militia of New Spain. México, May 3, 1766. A copy may be found in AGN:IO 6, fol. 77.

Bando conceding the *fuero* of provincials to *pardo* militiamen. México, December 24, 1767. A copy may be found in AGN:B 6, no. 87.

Bando conceding the *fuero* of provincials to the companies of urban cavalry of bakers, pork-butchers and tanners of Mexico. México, September 9, 1767. A copy may be found in AGN:B 6, no. 77.

Bando declaring the *fuero* of the militia of New Spain. México, May 11, 1795. A copy may be found in "Recuerdo sobre el cumplim.ᵗᵒ del Real Decreto de 9 de Febrero de 93 acerca del Fuero militar," AGN:IG 13 (1792–1794).

Bando publishing the royal decree of February 9, 1793. México, May 22, 1793. A copy may be found in "Cumplim.ᵗᵒ a[1] R.¹ Decreto y ōrn acompañatoria cortando disputas. . . ," AGN:IG 13 (1792–1794).

Beleña, Eusebio Bentura, comp. *Recopilación sumaria de todos los autos acordados de la real audiencia y sala del crimen de esta Nueva España, y providencias de su superior govierno.* 2 vols. México, 1787.

Circular order interpreting the royal decree of February 9, 1793. México, July 6, 1793. A copy may be found in "Cumplim.ᵗᵒ a[1] R.¹ Decreto y orn acompañatoria cortando disputas. . . ," AGN:IG 13 (1792–1794).

Colón de Larriátegui Ximénez de Embún, Félix. *Juzgados militares de España y sus Indias.* . . . 2a ed. corregida y aumentada. 4 vols. Madrid, 1786– 1796.

Escriche y Martín, Joaquín, comp. *Diccionario razonado de legislación y jurisprudencia.* . . . 3a ed. corr. y aum. . . . 3 vols. Madrid, 1847.

Gálvez, José de, marqués de Sonora. *Informe general que en virtud de real órden instruyó y entregó el exmo. sr. marqués de Sonora . . . al exmo. sr. virrey, frey d. Antonio Bucarely y Ursúa, con fecha de 31 de diciembre de 1771.* . . . México, 1867.

Instrucciones que los vireyes de Nueva España dejaron a sus sucesores. . . . México, 1867.

Instrucción que debe observar el subdelegado de ——— *para la creación de compañias sueltas de milicias en el distrito de su jurisdicción.* México, January 7, 1797. A copy may be found in "Documentacion sobre companias sueltas de milicias," AGN:IG 312 (1791–1797).

Novísima recopilación de las leyes de España [Los códigos españoles concordados y anotados (12 vols. Madrid, 1872–1873), Vols. VII–X].

Ordenanza de milicias provinciales de España. Madrid, 1734.

Ordenanzas de S.M. para el régimen, disciplina, subordinación, y servicio de sus exércitos. . . . 2 vols. Madrid, 1768.

Pérez y López, Antonio Xavier, comp. *Teatro de la legislación universal de España é Indias.* . . . 28 vols. Madrid, 1791–1798.

Real declaración sobre puntos esenciales de la Ordenanza de milicias provinciales de España, que ínterin se regla la formal, que corresponde á estos cuerpos, se debe observar como tal en todas sus partes. Madrid, 1767.

Reales ordenanzas para la dirección, régimen y gobierno del importante cuerpo de la minería de Nueva-España, y de su real tribunal general. Madrid, 1783.

Recopilación de leyes de los reinos de las Indias. . . . 5. éd. 4 vols. in 2. Madrid, 1841.

Reglamento para el régimen, gobierno y nueva planta de las compañías de milicias mixtas del seno que comprehende la provincia de Tampico y Pánuco, hasta el Río Guazacualco, costas laterales de Veracruz. México, 1793.

Reglamento para las milicias de infantería de la provincia de Yucatán, y Campeche. . . . Madrid, 1778.

Reglamento provisional para el cuerpo de milicias de caballería, que con el nombre de la Frontera de la colonia del Nuevo Santander, debe formarse en la jurisdicción de los valles y partido de Ríoverde. . . .México, 1793.

Reglamento provisional para el régimen, gobierno y nueva planta de las compañías de milicias de la costa del sur del reyno de Nueva España. . . . México, 1793.

Reglamento provisional para el régimen, gobierno y nueva planta de las milicias de la provincia de Tabasco. México, 1793.

Reglamento provisional para el régimen, gobierno, y nueva planta del cuerpo de infantería urbano del comercio de Puebla. México, [1793?]

Reglamento provisional para el régimen, gobierno y subsistencia del esquadrón urbano de caballería, que de las antiguas compañías de los tratantes de panadería, tocinería y curtiduría, se ha formado en esta capital. México, 1790.

Reglamento provisional para el régimen, gobierno y subsistencia del regimiento de infantería urbano del comercio de esta capital. México, 1793.

Reglamento provisional para el régimen y gobierno del cuerpo de milicias de caballería que con el nombre de Frontera de Sierra-Gorda ha de arreglarse en las jurisdicciones de Cadereyta, San Luis de la Paz, y presidio de Xalaca perteneciente á la de Mextitlán. . . . México, 1793.

Revillagigedo, Juan Vicente Güémez Pacheco de Padilla Horcasitas y Aguayo, conde de. *Instrucción reservada que el conde de Revilla Gigedo, dió a su sucesor en el mando, marqués de Branciforte.* . . . México, 1831.

Rodríguez de San Miguel, Juan Nepomuceno, comp. *Pandectas hispano-megicanas ó sea código comprensivo de las leyes . . . hasta el año de 1820.* 3 vols. Paris, 1852.

Royal decree defining the *fuero militar.* Aranjuez, February 9, 1793. This item may be found in "Cumplim.ᵗᵒ a[1] R.[1] Decreto y orn acompañatoria cortando disputas. . . ," AGN:IG 13 (1792–1794). It is also reproduced in part in the *Novísima recopilación de las leyes de España,* Lib. VI, tít. iv, ley 21.

Solórzano Pereira, Juan de. *Política indiana.* . . . 5 vols. Madrid and Buenos Aires, 1930.

Vicente y Caravantes, José. *Tratado de los procedimientos en los juzgados militares.* . . . Madrid, 1853.

Zamora y Coronado, José María, comp. *Biblioteca de legislación ultramarina en forma de diccionario alfabético.* . . . 6 vols. in 3. Madrid, 1844–1846.

Books and Articles

Aguirre Beltrán, Gonzalo. *La población negra de México, 1519–1810.* México, 1946.

Aiton, Arthur S. "Spanish Colonial Reorganization under the Family Compact," *The Hispanic American Historical Review,* XII (August, 1932), 269–280.

Bancroft, Hubert Howe. *History of Mexico.* 6 vols. San Francisco, 1883–1888.

Bayle, Constantino. *Los cabildos seculares en la América española.* Madrid, 1952.

Carmen Velázquez, María del. *El estado de guerra en Nueva España, 1760–1808.* México, 1950.

Casado Fernández-Mensaque, Fernando. "El Tribunal de la Acordada de Nueva España," *Anuario de estudios americanos,* VII (1950), 279–323.

Cavo, Andrés. *Los tres siglos de Méjico durante el gobierno español hasta la entrada del ejército trigarante.* . . . Jalapa, 1870.

Desdevises du Dezert, Gaston. "Les institutions de l'Espagne au XVIIIᵉ siècle," *Revue hispanique,* LXX (June-August, 1927), 1–554.

Diffie, Bailey W. *Latin-American Civilization: Colonial Period.* Harrisburg, 1945.

Dusenberry, William H. "Discriminatory Aspects of Legislation in Colonial Mexico," *The Journal of Negro History,* XXXIII (July, 1948), 284–302.

"El ejército de Nueva España a fines del siglo XVIII," *Boletín del archivo general de la nación,* IX (April-May-June, 1938), 236–275.

Fisher, Lillian Estelle. *The Intendant System in Spanish America.* Berkeley, 1929.

———————————— *Viceregal Administration in the Spanish-American Colonies.* Berkeley, 1926.

Fonseca, Fabián de, and Carlos Urrutía. *Historia general de real hacienda, escrita . . . por orden del virey, conde de Revillagigedo.* . . . 6 vols. México, 1845–1853.

Gazeta de México. Compendio de noticias de Nueva España desde principios del año de 1784 . . . por d. Manuel Antonio Valdez. . . . 44 vols. México, 1784–1821.

Howe, Walter. *The Mining Guild of New Spain and its Tribunal General, 1770–1821.* Cambridge, Massachusetts, 1949.

Humboldt, Alexander von. *Ensayo político sobre el reino de la Nueva España.* Sexta edición castellana. . . . 4 vols. and atlas. México, 1941.

Jane, Cecil. *Liberty and Despotism in Spanish America.* Oxford, 1929.

Kahle, Louis G. "The Spanish Colonial Judiciary," *The Southwestern Social Science Quarterly,* XXXII (June, 1951), 26–37.

Konetzke, Richard. "Estado y sociedad en las Indias," *Estudios americanos,* III (January, 1951), 33–58.

McAlister, Lyle N. "The Reorganization of the Army of New Spain, 1763–1767," *The Hispanic American Historical Review,* XXXIII (February, 1953), 1–32.

"La organización del ejército en Nueva España," *Boletín del archivo general de la nación,* XI (October-November-December, 1940), 617–663.

Parry, John H. *The Audiencia of New Galicia in the Sixteenth Century. A Study in Spanish Colonial Administration.* Cambridge, England, 1948.

———————————— *The Sale of Public Office in the Spanish Indies under the Hapsburgs* [University of California Publications, Ibero-Americana: 37]. Berkeley and Los Angeles, 1953.

Priestley, Herbert Ingram. *José de Gálvez, Visitor-General of New Spain (1765–1771).* Berkeley, 1916.

Rosenblat, Angel. *La población indígena de América desde 1492 hasta la actualidad.* Buenos Aires, 1945.

Smith, Robert S. "The Institution of the Consulado in New Spain," *The Hispanic American Historical Review,* XXIV (February, 1944), 61–83.

Smith, Robert S. *The Spanish Guild Merchant. A History of the Consulado, 1250–1700.* Durham, 1940.

Vance, John Thomas. *The Background of Hispanic-American Law. Legal Sources and Juridical Literature of Spain.* New York, 1942.

Villarroel, Hipólito. *México por dentro y fuera bajo el gobierno de los vireyes. . . . Manuscrito inédito que dá á luz por primer suplemento al tomo cuarto de la Voz de la pátria Carlos María de Bustamante. . . .* México, 1831.

Zorraquín Becú, Ricardo. *La organización judicial argentina en el periodo hispánico.* Buenos Aires, 1952.

Zúñiga y Ontiveros, Felipe de. *Calendario manual y guía de forasteros de México, para el año de 1789. . . .* México, [n. d.].

Index